Self-manag

Self-management: How it *Does* Work

Astrid Vermeer en Ben Wenting

REED BUSINESS INFORMATION, AMSTERDAM

Image design: Koos Heemskerk, Rijnsburg

Reed Business Information is part of Reed Business bv, Postbus 152, 1000 AD Amsterdam.

ISBN 978 90 352 4906 6
NUR 897, 807

Foreword

Back in 2005 when I had the first clear outlines for what would later become Buurtzorg Nederland, it was still not entirely clear what self-organization would look like in practice on a day-to-day basis. I was also used to using all sorts of 'management tools' that were needed to keep an organization manageable and monitorable. Although I had worked as a community health nurse in a self-managing team in the 1980s, I had the impression that a Balanced Score Card could nonetheless be very useful.

During the many conversations that I've had with Ben Wenting and Astrid Vermeer since the 1990s, we have continually viewed self-management and self-organization as guiding principles for the ideal organization. We saw that the negative consequences of 'management thinking' were placing more and more strain on professionals' everyday work. That in turn had immediate and serious consequences for the provision of care to patients.

For this reason, when I founded Buurtzorg Nederland in 2006 it went without saying that I would work with Ben and Astrid to create the supporting structure of this self-managing organization. Ten years later, we can reflect on an extremely successful collaboration and a development that has had a major impact both within the Netherlands and abroad.

This book makes it clear that self-management is not a gimmick, and that there's a lot more to it than just scrapping various layers of management. Self-organization and self-management call for a substantially different perspective on people and on how they are able to work together, day in and day out, to self-organise all the activities required for their everyday work. Excessive control, protocols and rules do not go together with having confidence in people who want to do their job as well as possible. This fantastic book outlines the practical necessities required to shape a more human organization. Ben and Astrid share their extensive knowledge and expertise on self-management in an accessible way, allowing the purpose of self-organization to come into its own: better service provision, and more meaningful work.

Jos de Blok
Director, Buurtzorg Nederland

Contents

Introduction

Following the publication of our first two Dutch-language books on self-managing organizations, we were regularly asked to write something on how to 'reconstruct' the hierarchical organization as a self-managing one. This book is the result.

Over the years we have been able to assist a large number of organizations in the transition from hierarchy to self-management, and we've gathered a wealth of knowledge and experience in the process. Self-management is a new form of structuring an organization and there's no single blueprint that is suitable for every organization.

The primary process and the confidence in the team members' knowledge and skills are central to self-management. These are used as the starting point to determine the best structure for the organization. Given that each area of work has its own specific characteristics, the form self-management takes can also vary considerably between organizations.

If, when implementing self-management, the company management employs these principles only partially or not at all and instead continues to think in a 'hierarchical' way, transition is often a difficult process. Over time people say that 'self-management doesn't work'. This is a great shame, because we have many examples which demonstrate that, when 'self-managing' is applied consistently, it *does* work.

And the effects are clearly visible: increased customer and employee satisfaction, improved co-operation between all stakeholders in the organization, and less overhead.

In *Self-management: How it* Does *Work*, we want to show how the organization can be structured in a self-managing way. We also explain what self-management means for the positions of manager, supporting staff, coach, and team member, and we give practical advice on how staff can shape their roles.

Finally, we examine the ways in which people can work together within the self-managing organization. We describe a solution-oriented communication method, because we think that this is the most appropriate style, and we elaborate on this in a number of concrete examples relating to everyday collaboration, meetings, and dealing with conflict.

Astrid Vermeer and Ben Wenting
June 2016
Email: zelfsturing@ivs-opleidingen.nl

1
The phenomenon of self-management

Political or social reform is rarely useful if it does not follow mental change.
– Gustave Le Bon –

Since around the time of the industrial revolution (i.e. the 19th century) we have organized the production of goods – and later service provision too – according to a hierarchical organizational model.

This model operates on the assumption that organizational processes can be managed using supervision and uniform regulations, thus allowing an organization to remain financially healthy and make a profit. This means that the logic of content-focused work processes and the professional opinions of those who carry out the primary process are regularly regarded as being of lesser importance. Task differentiation and specialization are often seen as a means of achieving good economic performance. The consequence of this can be that those who perform specialized sub-tasks lack a connection to the greater whole. This can result in the employee having an apathetic attitude, and losing a feeling of commitment to his or her work. Managers expect employees to demonstrate this commitment regardless, but a number of factors – including the way the work is organized – mean that it's difficult for them to muster.

In recent years it has become increasingly clear that traditional organizational forms are no longer satisfactory. The employees of today are well-educated professionals who are keen to use their knowledge and skills to perform their jobs well and improve the quality of their work.

Thus in recent years we have also seen regular initiatives in which, alongside the financial-economic motives, content-focused and/or sustainable motives are considered important too. Frederic Laloux covers these changes in detail in his book *Reinventing Organizations.*

In the Netherlands, the extreme specialization seen across the health care field stimulated Jos de Blok to establish his organization Buurtzorg Nederland. As a nurse, and later as manager and director, he experienced the negative consequences of the fragmentation of work first-hand, and made the decision to do things differently. His idea was that those who performed the work (in this case the nurses) were professionals and thus should once again be allowed to take responsibility for their work. This would be achieved by no longer fragmenting the work, and instead giving these professionals a complete package of tasks. This package would include all tasks required to properly organise the practical work. In addition, De Blok sees it as his responsibility as director to ensure that the preconditions required for the work have been met and the resources needed to carry it out are available. He also feels responsible for taking timely measures to ensure that the organization's financial health is maintained.

As a result the organization's primary process becomes the guiding principle, and the manager facilitates rather than controls.

Teams were put together in which the team members were collectively responsible for the results of their team. Every team member contributed to this. They organised the work together.

And so the self-managing, or self-organizing, team was born.

This new organizational form developed from a new way of thinking about the organization of the work and those who perform it. It is different from the traditional, hierarchical way of thinking. In the hierarchy, the thinking is done *for* the employees, and in self-organization it is done *with* them. This makes a world of difference in practice.

The section 'Effects of self-management' elaborates further on the consequences of introducing working with self-managing teams.

Many directors see the advantages of self-organization and think about moving their organization from a hierarchy to a form of self-management. With this book, we hope to give an impression of what is needed in order to make this transition possible.

In this first chapter we will discuss the phenomenon of self-management or self-organization. We use both of these names to describe the same principle.

WHY MOVE TO SELF-MANAGEMENT?

Before a director starts the transition to self-management, he might ask himself what he wants to achieve with it in his organization. Some directors look at the financial effects and see self-management as a way of getting the budget under control. This works to a certain extent, because as team members take responsibility for organizing their own work, the position of the operational supervisor often becomes superfluous. That can result in considerable savings.

But self-management is more than just scrapping the layer of operational managers and then telling the employees that they're self-directed and thus have responsibility for their own work.

That would ignore the principles on which self-organization is founded. The director can get started on self-management from a budget-conscious standpoint, but the effects are only really apparent if he also embraces the principles of self-organization.

Self-managing while continuing to think *for* the employees and control them from above is contradictory, and this contradiction will continue to play a role in the organization's ongoing development. Our experience is that in this situation, self-management can never really get off the ground.

When the management of the organization cannot support the principles underlying self-management, it's better to leave the hierarchy in place.

SELF-MANAGEMENT AS A MEANS AND NOT AN END IN ITSELF

So self-management develops, as we have seen, as the logical consequence of a different way of thinking about work and the role played by the employees who perform the work. Self-management is not a goal, but a means by which the content of the work, the primary process, takes a leading role in the organization.

There are many ways of applying self-organization, and they depend on the field of work. Self-management at Buurtzorg Nederland will look different to self-management at an educational institution, or in a biscuit factory; Buurtzorg has just one area of work, namely at-home care, and in practice this organization can be managed by a single director. In contrast, an occupational education facility usually consists of multiple areas, namely the different careers for which students are trained, and in addition to a director there are managers who are each responsible for a section. But at both of these organizations, the choices that are made are based on the requirements of the primary working process.

When self-management is seen as a means, and the organization is developed in keeping with the associated line of reasoning, in our view the self-managing organizational form is likely to succeed.

HOW DOES SELF-MANAGEMENT WORK?

In a self-managing organization, the team members are collectively responsible for the team result. Team decisions are made by consensus, so that each team member can also take individual responsibility for the agreements made. The manager has periodic discussions with the team about the vision, the frameworks within which the work is performed, and the organizational policy. The teams are assisted by a team coach who supports and advises the teams. The staff and supporting services advise the management and the teams and carry out tasks that are too specialized for the team. Properly functioning, user-friendly IT services ensure that the team members have sufficient information to enable them to organise their work.

This short definition naturally requires further explanation, and we will elaborate on the individual components in this and the following chapters.

FRAMEWORKS

When discussing self-management, the word 'framework' frequently comes up. Frameworks are important to self-organization, because they give the teams boundaries within which they can carry out their duties. The frameworks also indicate the minimum requirements necessary in order to keep the organization healthy.

Frameworks are generally initiated by the management of the organization, and are further discussed and determined in dialogue with the team members. This is an important factor, because when the team members can relate to the frameworks, they will also want to adhere to them.

Frameworks should be formulated in such a way that they allow sufficient space for the team to act. When the frameworks are too many and too rigid, they limit the degree of self-management. Frameworks must be something that assists with the work, not something that gets in the way. It is therefore important that the management holds an ongoing dialogue on frameworks with the teams and coaches, and is open to changes and adjustments.

Frameworks can be agreed in areas such as productivity, teamwork, educational requirements for team members, quality, customer satisfaction, regional distribution, resources used for work, and so on. However, a good social climate is also important, so frameworks around teamwork are essential too. For example, respecting differences within the team is a framework that can be agreed upon with regard to teamwork.

As we've already seen, it is therefore important to work with as few frameworks as possible – but relevant ones. These may differ for each duty, department, or area of work. The frameworks also reflect an organization's mission. A home care organization, for example, might agree that people should be able to live 'just like they would at home'.

QUALITY ASSURANCE

One common criticism of the way a self-organization operates is: 'But what about quality assurance? You can't just leave that to the people who do the work! They lack the knowledge and the overview ...' This is usually followed by arguments that show that there is little or no confidence in the quality of the professionals' knowledge and skills. But one of the pillars of self-organization is precisely that: to have *trust* in professionals; after all, they've trained for their jobs. The same applies to quality assurance. Perhaps the teams are not (yet) used to thinking in terms of quality standards and making quality standards concrete, but that doesn't mean that they don't have any idea of what good quality looks like.

The management and supporting services are tasked with facilitating the teams' efforts to assure quality, using quality frameworks and formats which team members can implement in practice (but only if the team members need these – because who says that they can't organise them for themselves?).

If the manager sees signs that a team's quality level is somewhat lacking, then during a meeting with the team he[1] might ask something like, 'What do you need in order to ensure quality in your team?' If it turns out that the team can't give a concrete answer right away, the manager can help them by providing examples from other teams or by referring them to a quality officer if one is available. The team coach can also help the team to come up with concrete quality agreements. Quality assurance might mean creating a checklist to be completed before the finished product is sent to the customer, using a good reporting system which describes the client's health, or introducing a pupil monitoring system.

When developing any type of quality system, it is extremely important that those who have to work with the system feel that it is a useful and workable one – otherwise it's counterproductive.

NO MORE THAN NECESSARY

In a traditional organization, people aim to control and monitor systems and to develop protocols that make monitoring possible. This results in countless rules and procedures that everyone is required to follow. Many people are required – not only to develop these rules, but also to ensure that all rules are followed.

[1] The pronouns 'he' and 'she' are used interchangeably.

In a self-managing organization we try to do what helps us to achieve the team results. Part of this involves getting rid of those aspects which don't help with this and are therefore unnecessary.

When an organization makes the transition from hierarchy to self-organization, it is quickly apparent that the many rules that were previously required are a hindrance to the teams. It's important to work together to determine whether a rule assists in carrying out the primary process. If this is not the case, it can be scrapped. Experience shows that sometimes a great number of rules can be scrapped; in one organization with two thousand employees, all rules and protocols were inventoried as part of the preliminary phase towards self-management. There turned out to be twelve hundred of these, ranging from regulations on long-service anniversaries right through to quality control. In collaboration with the employees, the rules were then examined to determine which ones were considered relevant; they came up with three hundred!

Disposing of unnecessary rules and regulations obviously makes it much easier to gain a clear view of the organization. In addition, it frees up a lot of time because there are no redundant operations that have to be carried out. This time can then be used for essential tasks such as caring for clients or teaching pupils.

DIFFERENCES ARE OK

Once there are clear frameworks within which the teams can work and can make their own decisions, we slowly but surely begin to see differences develop between teams. Managers who think in terms of control are annoyed by and disapprove of this, because the difference between what is 'right' and what is 'wrong' is no longer obvious.

However, when viewed with a focus on the primary process, differences between teams are sometimes necessary in order to be able to respond to customers' needs. This is, after all, one of the objectives of self-organization. If a home care team is active in a neighbourhood that's home to many young, employed people, it will require a different dynamic with different team agreements from those of a team working in an area where many elderly people live.

CONSEQUENCES OF SELF-MANAGEMENT FOR THE VARIOUS FUNCTION GROUPS

Self-organization doesn't just have consequences for the way in which work processes are organized; it also affects the way in which the various employees perform their work. This section briefly considers what working in a self-organization, as compared to working in a hierarchical setting, means for each specific function group.

The following chapters explore what it means to work in a self-organization in more depth.

The management

In a hierarchical setting, one of the management's tasks is 'monitoring the results and the quality'. Each manager monitors the employees that he manages. Some hierarchies have as many as five levels. In a self-managing organization, the team members monitor themselves and each other. In a hierarchy, the operational manager is the one who manages the execution and thus also monitors the team's results. When this task is assigned to the team members, the operational manager's task will probably disappear. Even more than that – it *should* disappear, because it doesn't work well when both the team members and the manager are responsible for the results.

Further development of the self-managing organization also shows the extent to which the existence of middle management is justified; depending on the area of work and the number of teams, it should be clear whether or not this layer of management is functional. Organizations that have multiple areas of work, or that work in different regions, often choose to appoint a manager for each area of work. For example, a retail chain might appoint a manager for each product group, with a manager at the top who directs all of them. In the case of a health care organization offering both intramural and extramural care, there might be an Intramural Care manager *and* an Extramural Care manager, and a director who works together with the two managers to determine the course of the entire organization. But there are also organizations that choose to scrap the position of manager, and then the regional or product managers form a self-managing team that is responsible for the overall organization.

The manager's task is threefold:
1 He ensures that the organization's vision and mission is carried out both internally and externally.
2 He facilitates the teams; what do the team members need in order to be able to do their jobs? This might include the frameworks discussed above, in addition to things such as team budgets, bringing in experts, housing, educational opportunities and ICT facilities.
3 He has final responsibility for his service or organization, meaning that he sometimes has to make difficult decisions – for example, at times when the team members don't adhere consistently to a framework, or an employee doesn't carry out his work properly.

One of the biggest changes for a manager in a self-managing organization is the change in thinking, from *for* the team members to *with* the team members.

In other words: the manager no longer assumes that he knows what's good for others, but instead asks what others need.

Supporting services

In a hierarchy, many supporting or staff services are tasked with developing protocols and regulations, making the primary process (more) manageable. They also advise line workers according to their specific field.

In the self-directed organization, development of rules and the like will occur less often because controlling the organizational processes has become less important.

Staff services will need to focus more on developing diverse solutions for problems that at first glance appear to be the same. In the self-organization, team members need to be able to respond adequately to their customers' needs. This may well mean that a solution works better for one team than for another. Another solution must then be found for that other team. Fire brigade teams may well encounter the same problems, but teams in the city experience a different dynamic when putting out fires to those in rural areas.

Employees in staff functions must have a very customer-friendly attitude so that they can 'think along' on the specific solutions that a team needs.

The team members

A lot changes for team members when they begin self-managing. When working in a hierarchy, the manager makes the decisions and therefore the employee bears little responsibility. Each employee has an individual relationship with the manager; she receives assignments from him and doesn't have final responsibility for these.

In a self-managing organization the team members are collectively responsible for the team result; this requires the team members to have a co-operative attitude. It's also important that the team members use a solution-oriented communication style so they don't get bogged down in problems, but instead make agreements that move them forward.

Given that the team members are jointly responsible for the team results, decisions are made by consensus (there is no objection), so that the decisions are workable for every team member and they can each feel responsible for them. For this reason, a good team meeting is one of the pillars of a self-managing team.

The team members also look after each other. Amongst other things, this means looking at how each person can work in a way that suits their personal qualities. It also means that when a colleague fails to fulfil her commitments, the team members discuss it with each other. It's not always easy; in the past the manager always did this, so the team members haven't yet developed a routine for it.

Finally, we want to mention that working in a self-managing team requires a certain entrepreneurial behaviour from the team members; if you see that your team's productivity is declining, you will need to take action to enable your team to work more cost-effectively.

The team coach

In a self-managing organization, the teams can usually call on a team coach to assist them with self-managing. The team coach has no say on the topics discussed within the team, and is not part of the team.

The coach is there to assist both the team as a whole and the individual team members, so it's important that she is always a good and objective sounding board for all team members in all situations. The more the coach maintains her objective, non-judgmental working method, the better she can help the team members to together find good solutions to the problems.

In order to provide good support to a team, the coach must be able to provide a safe environment in which the team feels free to discuss mistakes and to ask any question at all.

THE WORKS COUNCIL IN A SELF-ORGANIZATION

In a hierarchy, employees generally have little influence on decisions made within the organization and the organization must establish a Works Council so that employees can have their say. In a Works Council, representatives chosen by the employees discuss organizational decisions with the management, as well as discussing employees' interests such as working conditions.

Some may wonder whether a Works Council is necessary in a well-organized self-managing organization. Buurtzorg Netherlands doesn't think so. The organization has demonstrably given so much control to the teams that teams have sufficient opportunity to influence their own working conditions. For this reason, Buurtzorg Netherlands has been granted an exemption from the Works Councils Act.

It may be that a Works Council is still desirable in order to influence the manager on issues such as vision, policy and organizational change, but the council's role as representation in the workplace is no longer required.

PITFALLS

We have touched on some of the pitfalls of setting up a self-managing organization in the text above, but here is a list of the most common.

- Thinking for others, unasked; co-operation amongst all employees is part of the power of self-managing. Each employee, in his specific role, adds what's needed in order to make or deliver the product or service as well as possible. When one person decides what's best for another, the other's professionalism is ignored. This causes resentment and interferes with co-operation.
- Allowing a hierarchy to develop within the team; team members perform organizational tasks and sometimes a team member plays the 'boss' in this area. This leads to a loss of equality and the self-managing team loses strength.
- Wanting to organise and control too much; we are so used to coming up with rules that we find it hard to stop doing it in a self-organization. But doing so deprives the teams of a lot of space to make their own decisions, meaning that self-management can't get off the ground properly and can even be supressed.
- Too few facilities; teams need facilities to carry out their duties. The manager needs to provide these. Without facilities like sufficient leeway and good information provision, team members can't influence their team results. This can therefore also be a reason why self-management never really gets off the ground.

EFFECTS OF SELF-MANAGEMENT

We will round off this chapter with the positive effects of self-organization.

One of the main effects seen when self-management works well is an enormous increase in employee satisfaction. Employees thrive when they have control over their work and are able to be creative in finding solutions to difficult work situations. 'Finally I'm allowed to do the thing I studied for', is a frequently-heard saying.

Managers are often stunned by the professionalism that team members show when carrying out their duties. This naturally has a direct impact on *customer satisfaction.* Customers feel that their voices are being heard more clearly, and their individual needs can be taken into account.

Self-management has positive organizational effects too. Less time is required for monitoring and management tasks, meaning a considerable *saving on overhead costs*. This in turn means that fewer staff are required, and the reduction in regulations make it easier to gain a clear overview of the organization. The lines of communication are shorter, leaving more time for other, more substantive tasks.

Basically, it may well be worthwhile for everyone ...

The **effects** of self-management
- Increased employee satisfaction
- Increased customer satisfaction
- Saving on overhead costs
- Shorter lines of communication
- Fewer rules and regulations

2
From hierarchy to self-management

It always seems impossible until it's done.
– Nelson Mandela –

And then one (fine) day the decision is made to move the organization to self-management. But that's just the start – because how do you do that? How do you manage to 'turn over' the entire organization? And it's not always easy. You don't just need a new shape and structure – the members of the organization also have to conduct themselves differently.

We have observed that it is really helpful for the management to think and act in accordance with the principles of self-organization, right from the moment that the decision to change structure is made. This ensures that the entire transition comes across as credible. In addition, we have seen that this gives momentum to the entire change, meaning that the new organization is achieved more quickly.

Moving towards self-organization without (yet) having embraced the associated mindset can be compared to building a house on quicksand.

Employees – and managers – get confused; what's expected of me now, and what isn't? What can I influence, and what can't I?

In this chapter we describe the aspects that play a role in this transition and how they can be handled in practice.

COMMITMENT TO THE ORGANIZATION'S VISION AND STRUCTURE

Before taking concrete further steps, it's important to discuss self-management and its consequences with the other members of the organization.

These other members will include the other managers (middle and lower frameworks), those who carry out the work, and the supporting services.

A good self-management introduction process requires that all members of the organization take part, and part of this is also that everyone is involved in opinion-forming.

Most employees experience self-management as a good organizational structure. However, there will be employees who don't like it, because it relies greatly on co-operation skills, willingness to contribute, and taking responsibility. This can be taken into account to a certain extent. The management is in the position to determine the course of the organization, and choosing the organizational structure is part of this. Obtaining the commitment of all employees is thus probably not an option.

If the majority of the employees who carry out the work have serious objections, it's probably sensible to add a few additional steps and to take measures based on these objections, so that the employees *are* motivated to work for a self-managing organization. By taking stakeholder views into account, you as the management show that you actively want to work in accordance with self-organization principles.

Managers, particularly those who directly supervise those who carry out the work, note that one of the consequences of self-management is that some of their duties are scrapped or become the responsibility of the self-managing team. This usually means that the managers' positions disappear. A good redundancy scheme, or for example moving these staff to the primary process, then becomes an option. It should therefore be expected that this group will not be highly motivated to work on creating a self-managing organization.

BLUEPRINT OR DEVELOPMENT MODEL?

There are basically two ways to bring about organizational change: a blueprint, and a development model. This is not the place to go into these options in detail, but in the context of developing self-organization we would nonetheless like to devote a small amount of space to them.

In many situations a blueprint for implementing the new organization is created. Following analysis, a timetable is outlined and the plan is executed step by step; the members of the organization comply with the blueprint. When working with a blueprint, people often fail to take into account employees' wishes on the various steps that are taken. As a result, the employees are not committed to the changes. A detailed plan also allows little or no room to respond to situations that arise during the implementation phase.

Conversely, with self-organization the intention is to develop a dialogue between the different members of the organization so they can discuss the best way of achieving the 'new' organization. The employees who carry out the primary process play an equally important role as the managers and support staff.

For this reason, we think that the development model is a better one; the members of the organization are included in developing the plan, and the impact of each step is considered throughout the process. This allows the current situation to be taken into account at every stage, and the process of change is completely tailored to the situation.

PILOT

It may be a good decision to break away a section of the organization and to set this up as self-organizing as discussed earlier. This section can then be used to explore what does and doesn't work, what team members need to know and to be able to do, what is superfluous and what can be ignored. The positive and negative experiences here can be used as a basis for developing self-management in the rest of the organization. Staff are sometimes more motivated by their peers than by the management, which may be an additional incentive.

The advantage of using a pilot is that the inevitable teething problems will only affect a small segment of the organization. In addition, in a relatively small group it is often easier to look for good ways to solve a problem. Certain problems will always arise when introducing self-management (for example setting up a good IT system; you can only know whether it works well by testing it in practice), but for the most part you will already have tested the best solution during the pilot phase.

It's important to carry out the pilot in a section of the organization that is more or less representative of the whole; otherwise it may be difficult to apply the experience gained to the rest of the organization. If such a section is not available (and can't be created), then our advice would be to not use a pilot.

The supporting services should be involved in the pilot too, so that the consequences that self-management will have for them are also clear.

During the pilot phase, the experiences and results will be discussed regularly and the requirements of the plan for implementing self-management throughout the entire organization will become clearer.

PHASED IMPLEMENTATION

When a management team chooses to implement self-management in phases, in our view that means that, in co-operation with the stakeholders, you are going to look at how the organization can be 'tilted'. Phased implementation also considers how the work can be carried out properly at the same time, without the clients or production process being overly affected by the process of change. It could be compared to planning a home renovation: which things is it logical to do first, and which later, so you don't have to do things twice? It's obviously not a good idea to first lay a beautiful floor and then to break down a wall. It's therefore also not a good idea to dismantle the operational framework first and then instruct the teams to self-manage, while failing to offer any facilities which would enable the team members to manage themselves.

What does work

- Management preparing well on the theme of 'self-organization', and endorsing the principle.

- Contact with team members about the consequences.
- Setting up the facilities well.
- Contact with the team members regarding the point at which the team will be able to self-manage.
- Starting with the teams that can/want to do this. The other teams will follow at the time of their choice.
- Continuing to assess the developments, and solving problems in the spirit of self-management.

The last of these is something that never stops; as mentioned earlier, an organization is a living thing, because constant societal and organizational changes mean that people constantly need to adapt.

SWITCHING OVER ALL AT ONCE

Some organizations choose a particular date to switch the organization from a traditional hierarchical one to a self-organization. This method can work well too.

To switch over successfully, a development plan should be drawn up with a step by step outline of how the requirements for self-organization will be realised. We deliberately call it a development plan and not an implementation plan, because there needs to be room to deviate from the plan and to respond adequately to new insights while working towards self-organization. By creating an implementation plan, you run the risk that you will want to implement the plan just as it was designed and you won't leave yourself much room to deviate from it, even if it's necessary.

Right from the beginning, there should be room in the development plan for making distinctions between how self-organization is implemented for departments and for teams. The development plan is thus more about the steps that you take and the development of facilities that need to be provided, than about the content of the transition. Sometimes, for example, an implementation plan needs to prescribe how the training budget should be distributed among the different teams and team members. But the power of self-organization is precisely that the entity (the department and/or team) itself can decide what's needed. A department that is undergoing incredible development needs to be able to use training budgets in a different way from a department that has stabilized.

In addition, in many organizations we see that the preparations are made with a working group consisting of people who work in teams, support employees, and managers. This is of course done on a voluntary basis. However, this way of working can have a negative effect. People who want to join the working group are invariably people who are enthusiastic about self-management. This means that those who are not so keen are not heard, although their critical (and perhaps even unmotivated) attitude means that they could bring up many issues which would otherwise remain underexposed. Working with a select group to prepare for the change excludes people who have just as much interest as anyone else does in the organization being structured well. Commonly-heard cries include: 'I'm really not impressed with everything that they've once again come up with for us', or 'They have no idea what actually happens here in the workplace, they never ask us what we think ...' 'It's always the same ones who get to have a say ...'

At the start of the transition, organizations often take a baseline measurement: what does everyone think of self-organization at the moment, and what should it deliver to you? Once self-management has been in effect for a while, a new measurement is taken to see whether people have changed their opinion.

However, if there is no concrete image of self-organization (and there isn't one, because almost no-one has worked in a truly well-functioning self-organization), then what the baseline is measuring is in fact unclear. If it should also happen that there have already been many reorganizations in recent years, then the picture will be rather negative: 'the nth change that won't actually do anything', 'well, at least it can't get any worse'.

If you are curious about the organization members' experience of the points before and after the implementation, then ask questions about what people would like to see achieved through the introduction of self-organization, and measure whether this has been successful after several months (or even years). This makes it easier for management to steer and to achieve objectives.

PROJECT MANAGER

During the implementation process, some organizations work with a project manager. There are two types: a project manager who is part of the organization, and one who has been brought in from outside. The question is, of course, 'Why would you choose which option, and what tasks do you give to an internal and/or external project manager?'

Let's start with the internal project manager. This is again a relevant question: what needs to be achieved by appointing an internal project manager to introduce self-management?

She could, for example, take care of work for the management. As described earlier, it is important to consult the teams when structuring the organization further. This takes time, and a project manager can do a lot of the preparatory work required. A condition of this is that the project manager is neutral, and limits herself to merely collecting information – assessing the information is the management's responsibility.

The internal project manager may also be tasked with documenting the managers' discussions with each other and with others, with following the project, and where necessary advising on and initiating subsequent steps.

In addition, although the internal project manager has no say in how things are done, it is certainly a good idea to appoint a competent person who can be a fully-fledged partner in discussions. Otherwise the project manager position is limited to secretarial work. There's nothing wrong with this, but in that case it would be better and cheaper to have a secretary carry out the tasks.

We do not see an internal project manager as being essential to the success of introducing self-management.

Roughly the same applies to the external project manager. When an external project manager is used, it's important to know what needs to be achieved by hiring the consultant. As a rule this person will be someone who, in the directors' eyes, brings added value. The advantage of an external project manager may be that she brings a lot of expertise from organizations that are already further along in the process of their development towards self-management.

The external project manager will preferably work together with the management according to the development model, whereby various options for each subsequent activity are jointly examined, following which the management makes a decision.

ESTABLISHING CONDITIONS AND FACILITIES

When the decision is made to move to self-management, establishing conditions and setting up facilities is essential.

Concrete agreements on team results

If a team manages itself based on results, then there's no getting around describing those results. When you know what you need to achieve, it's easier to determine the actions that need to be taken in order to reach your goal.

The expected results can be found in the frameworks (for example: the team needs to hit a productivity level of at least 65%). But the organization's vision or mission can indicate the team's goal/result too: nursing and caring for people at home in region X.

Frameworks

It's important to develop frameworks for teams during the implementation process, in order to determine the margins within which the teams can operate.

The frameworks are usually initiated by the manager and agreed on with the teams, but teams can also indicate the information that they need to know in order to know how much leeway they have and what they think they will need in order to be able to achieve their results.

Monitoring and influencing results

Team members must be able to see the impact that their actions and activities have on the team result; this allows them to make effective adjustments. In a traditional organization, the manager receives the data and gives the team assignments based on these.

It works differently in a self-managing organization. Here, the team members are responsible for the result, and so they need to be able to influence it, but they are only able to do this if they receive direct feedback on the effects of their activities; if the team members draw up a more efficient schedule that has less 'waiting time' between appointments, they can serve more clients and thus achieve higher productivity. This immediate feedback motivates them to do even better.

For this reason, a good IT system needs to be developed that enables teams to have this information at their disposal. Such a system should give access not only to productivity-related data, but also data related to absenteeism, available budgets, quality monitoring procedures, and procedures for discussing co-operation within the team.

The team members can also be asked what information they need in order to be able to influence their work process.

Time to carry out team tasks

In a self-organization, the team members perform organizational tasks in addition to their practical work. These should be anticipated prior to the team beginning to operate as a self-managing team. Tasks that are necessary in order to organise the work might include making schedules, making visits to clients, team meetings to discuss the team's progress, discussing the quality of the work, solving day-to-day problems, and making plans for the future. In a hierarchy, the manager is the one responsible for these overhead tasks and has plenty of time for these. The team members will obviously also need time to carry out these tasks, and this time needs to be provided before the team is self-managing.

A review must be made of which tasks will be assigned to the team, roughly how much time these will take, and what this will mean for the staff.

Training

Working in a self-organization calls for different qualities than working in a hierarchy. Team members have to be able to communicate with each other in the team on an equal basis, to be good at consulting each other, make decisions by consensus, and approach each other with regard to incompetent conduct and agreements that have not been fulfilled. In addition, people have to learn to think in terms of results and to find ways of influencing the results.

Managers of self-managing teams must be able to ask good questions, allow accountability for tasks to rest with the team members, and be able to facilitate the team rather than sorting things out for them. Supporting services must be customer-friendly and provide support to the primary process.

Usually (in a traditional organization) the management or the HR department is the one to determine the way in which everyone can best master the new skills. Usually a training plan is then created, which involves each group of staff going through the process whether they think it will be useful or not. After all, uniformity is important for keeping change under control.

With self-organization, however, the starting point is what the team members need in order to be able to do their work properly. The skills which are lacking and the way in which these can be taught are then examined based on these requirements.

This might mean organizing training sessions, but some people learn better by watching others, reading books or watching films. The times at which training is useful may also vary. One team might prefer to undergo training when self-managing is first implemented, while another may prefer to work in the 'new' way for a while first so that they can ask specific questions based on their experiences.

For this reason, when introducing self-organization it's important to provide different ways for the staff to master new skills, and which allow everyone the freedom to do this in their own way and in their own time.

This will mean that the staff will be more motivated to learn, which makes it easier to retain the material. It's also more attractive in financial terms, because only the training that's actually needed will be carried out and team members are not taxed with knowledge that they don't need.

Changes to employment contracts

Different requirements are imposed on staff members in a self-managing organization. People who are new to working in a self-managing organization are often not aware of the difference or of what's expected of them, which can cause a few hiccups with teamwork. It's obviously important to make the expectations clear during the recruitment process, but they are even clearer when the employment contract contains a clause setting them out. When the new employee signs the contract, it can then be assumed that he knows what's expected of him, and the requirements can also be addressed with him. For example, the following agreements might be made:

- as a team member, you are responsible for the content of the work, productivity, work practices, quality and collaboration;
- team decisions are made by consensus.

This type of clause not only makes it easier to address issues with each other, but the team members know what to expect when they start work on a self-organizing team.

Developing facilities together with 'users'

In all of the aforementioned facilities, it is very important that the team members – that is, the users – experience the facilities as something that helps them with their work and not as a millstone. If the team members are not able to work with the tools and see no added value in carrying out their duties, they will simply try to avoid the facility concerned.

IT system developers, in particular, have the tendency to put together fabulous systems which aren't very user-friendly. They forget that the average employee in an organization has no IT background. A system will only be used if it is simple and logical to use – but this may mean that it looks hideous to the designer's eyes. If that's the case, then so be it. The IT developer (and all other support staff in the organization) will have to be more customer-friendly – and their customer is the team.

The other facilities, too, need to be established in consultation with the team members. Simply put, an organization is a dynamic entity and things change frequently. This means that the discussion between management and teams about performance and features is an ongoing dialogue.

Service centre

If the primary organization is able to start working as a self-organization, it may be useful to set up a service centre where the team members can go with their questions. The service centre ensures that the question gets to the right person. We will return to this in chapter 4.

REORGANIZING TEAMS AND TEAM STRUCTURE

The introduction of self-organizing teams provides the opportunity to review the structure of the organization and the way the teams are organised. Are the right staff to achieve the team result placed together on each team? Are the duties classified under the right service or department? Are the regions divided up logically? Are the specialists in the right place in the organization or assigned to the teams?

The team members know the answers to these questions better than anyone else does. Some people have been irritated for years by the fact that, for example, they have to work with colleagues who have been assigned to other teams even though they work together on a daily basis.

When reorganizing the organization, the number and type of managers required should also be considered, as well as what the changes will mean for the supporting services. How does this service fit logically into a self-organization?

Thinking about this, carrying out discussions, and restructuring the organization and the teams may take quite some time. After all, the process is actually the establishment of a new organization ...

Plans for a potential new structure can be discussed with stakeholders, and ultimately the management/board must determine the final design.

SCRAPPING UNNECESSARY RULES

When redesigning the organization, the current rules and protocols can also be examined to see which ones are useful to the successful completion of the work. Unnecessary, and even counterproductive, rules can thus be spotted at the same time.

The aim of a self-organization is to achieve goals and to facilitate the process of achieving them. Everyone knows from experience that it's much more pleasant to work with as few rules as possible; it allows you to focus on the core task. Police officers have complained for years about the enormous amount of bureaucracy that keeps them busier filling out forms than catching crooks.

So the aim is to have as few rules as possible. Or to put it positively: only rules that help with carrying out the work.

Incidentally, this is something that continues long after self-management is introduced, because there is always a tendency to develop new rules and guidelines to satisfy the need for control. In many cases it's enough to come up with an individual solution to a problem, without needing to create another new rule. The self-managing organization only really develops once 'control thinking' has taken a back seat.

THE MANAGER AS TEAM COACH?

Organizations often retrain team leaders as team coaches. The transition to self-organization means that these staff are superfluous to requirements and need to either find a new position within the company or be made redundant. The latter is not always appealing to the organization due to the sometimes high severance payments required, so such staff are offered a team coach position. It's an obvious choice – however, some caveats should be given.

In some cases, *all* team leaders are moved to the team coach position. The team coach coaches the same number of teams (one to three, on average) as she once led. Given that the team leader's tasks are now the team's responsibility, and the team coach only does something for the team when it's necessary, it's clear that the team coach will have a great deal of free time. Her experience as team leader means that she knows exactly what's going on in the team, so she will interfere with the team more than necessary (and usually unasked). If she wasn't the most democratic team leader, then she won't make any secret of her opinion and will let the team know exactly how best they should work. This obviously undermines the natural process of achieving self-organization. The team may well even oppose the coach's interference and try to exclude her.

This situation can be avoided by appointing as few team coaches as possible, and not allowing the coach to coach teams for which she was earlier the team leader.

The second danger that lies in wait is that the team leader who becomes a team coach may not have the talent to perform the role well. The position of team leader is a completely different one to that of team coach, requiring different skills. A team leader manages the team and therefore has an opinion on the content, she bears final responsibility, and she monitors how the work is performed.

Conversely, the team coach has *no* opinion on the content (more on this in Chapter 5) and certainly doesn't make decisions for the team. She is not responsible, and therefore doesn't monitor anything.

Some team coaches who were previously team leaders can't (or don't want to) unlearn this, and are therefore not suitable for the position of coach.

Team leaders who have always led the team democratically have a good chance of being successful team coaches. Even in the hierarchical era, such team leaders probably endorsed all the principles that are important in self-organization, and always had faith in their employees' qualities.

It is therefore important to ensure that a good selection procedure is developed to enable the appointment of good team coaches.

MANAGERS ALSO ESSENTIALLY IN FAVOUR OF SELF-ORGANIZATION

During the implementation process, it is important to look carefully at the way that the manager will carry out his duties in the new situation. The Board decides to move to self-organization, but it is very far removed from the teams. If the managers directly under Board level are not wholeheartedly in support of self-organization principles, they will continue to manage in a hierarchical way and will cause disruption. It is often assumed that such managers are just doing what they should be doing, but in practice we see many examples in which it was clear that the manager was no fan of self-management and undermined the system in his dealings with the teams.

If the consequences of introducing self-management are discussed with the manager, there will come a point when he himself has to answer the question of whether he can and will work in that way. Managers at that level have usually very deliberately chosen to work as a manager in the hierarchical sense of the word, and now they find themselves being asked to think not *for* the teams, but *with* the teams. Instead of being the 'boss', they are now asked to take an instrumental, facilitating position. This is often far from the image that they have of themselves.

If the manager in question doesn't see himself as a facilitator, it would be best for him to look for another working environment where he can manage in a way that suits him.

EVERYONE IN A SELF-MANAGING TEAM?

Self-management is a means of achieving an objective. If having a number of staff working together creates added value for both the client and the team members, then self-management is a good choice – but if there's no added value, then there's also no reason to make the team self-managing.

This seems to be true of teams consisting of employees who all have their own case load and manage their own diaries. Team coaches are often put together on their own self-managing team, but they have no idea what they should manage together. Ultimately there is no shared responsibility, no common goal and no interdependence (except perhaps for sharing experiences and advising each other regarding the quality of their work, but that's no foundation for working in a self-organizing context).

The same applies to other specialists who work for teams throughout the entire organization, with no shared objective and, thereby, responsibility.

In such cases it would be more logical to place the staff under a manager with whom each individual can discuss their progress.

It may be useful to organize intervision (peer-to-peer coaching) within a team of specialists where people ask and give advice to each other on substantive and methodological matters. One pitfall here is that people try to agree on the solution to the problem. They then run the risk of agreeing on uniform rules, while the strength of having a specialist with her own caseload is precisely that she has the ability to identify specific solutions to specific problems. Intervision should thus be focused on increasing quality and the employees increasing insight into their own actions.

Other forms

Sometimes a number of staff need to work on a clearly-defined temporary assignment. This might be, for example, preparing an annual report, developing an advertising campaign, or developing a new product. The staff involved then form a self-managing team for the duration of the project. In principle, the same 'rules of play' (perhaps with a few modifications) apply to these teams as to teams that are always self-managing.

When putting the team together, the content of the work is used as a starting point for organization (in this case the 'project' is the primary process).

So: what is the goal to be achieved (for example, producing an annual report)? Which staff members have a task to perform towards this goal? What powers do they have? What facilities do they need in order to achieve the goal? Who is in a position to offer these facilities? When does the task need to be completed?

The temporary self-managing team ensures that the work is done and discusses its progress with the client. (In this case the client is most likely the management/Board.)

The same applies to specialists who are attached to a team; this is a common situation in the health care sector. In health care there are teams of group leaders, youth welfare workers, psychiatric nurses, sheltered housing supervisors, etc., working together in self-managing teams to care for, assist and/or nurse a group of clients. The remedial educationalist, psychologist or psychiatrist, for example, has regular contact to discuss and make adjustments to working methods. These specialists are sometimes permanently attached to the self-managing team for a certain percentage FTE, working to support the team with the methodology used rather than the execution of the work itself. This means that they don't carry out any team tasks, and don't participate in rosters, holiday schedules etc. They are under the direct supervision of a manager.

The specialist then shares responsibility for treatment and counselling methodology with the teams for which he works.

SELF-MANAGEMENT MEANS A COMPLETE CULTURAL CHANGE!

Self-management represents a different way of thinking about collaboration; instead of giving orders and monitoring their progress, more emphasis is placed on personal and team responsibility. It's a collaboration method based on trust and good mutual consultation. It also calls for a direct approach culture when it comes to results, quality, development, and being customer-oriented. There is a shift from individual responsibility for tasks to group responsibility for tasks. All of this is often experienced as a cultural change – which is usually what it is.

Self-management requires more flexibility. It aims to achieve compromise, take each other into account more, and to address each other regarding quality and working processes, increased personal initiative, entrepreneurial behaviour and the like.

The team members usually already possess the skills required for this different way of working, but don't always have to draw on them for their work. Prior to self-organization, they applied these qualities to running the sports club, organizing events, providing voluntary care, and 'simply' keeping the family going. People appreciate being able to put these qualities to use at work too.

In our view, it's not a true cultural change; it's more about placing a different value on the work and the employees' qualities. So ... don't place too much emphasis on it, but make use of what people already do well.

This doesn't need to be announced with big parties, cool presents, conferences presented by roller-skating MCs, and films in which the autocratic tracksuit-wearing director suddenly shouts that he's seen the light.

If tasks are then assigned in the same top-down, managing, monitoring way, it shows that the management hasn't understood much about the process. They would then be better off keeping the money for those sorts of treats in their wallets.

3
The manager

Be the change that you want to see in the world.
– Mahatma Ghandi –

LETTING GO AND FACILITATING

By now it will be clear that the teams are responsible for how their work is carried out: qualitatively and quantitatively. For the manager, this means that he will perform his role differently, while still bearing final responsibility: he's responsible for agreeing on the framework, but no longer interferes with the operational work process.

It's not easy to let go of something that's been part of your daily routine for years. And what exactly are you meant to let go of? The trick is not to pay attention to how the work is carried out any more, as long as the team is operating within the frameworks. You also have to trust that the team will call for your assistance if it's needed. In addition, you make a deal with the team that they will give you regular progress reports.

Managers sometimes continue to manage and set strict rules because they're scared of chaos and anarchy in the team. However, experience shows that as the frameworks become broader and are agreed on with the team members, there isn't any chaos. The team members are then able to feel fully responsible for what happens within the team, and will do everything they can to ensure that things go well.

If the manager is able to leave the managerial behaviour behind and instead focus on facilitating the work process, then self-organization has a good chance of success.

HOW DOES THE MANAGER DEVELOP FRAMEWORKS?

At a certain point it will happen: the manager will be expected to come up with workable frameworks. Many managers are apprehensive about developing them, because it's something that really doesn't happen in a hierarchy. In a hierarchy, rules are thought up and projects are assigned, but frameworks within which the team members can make their own decisions are new to most managers.

Where do you start? And when is something a framework and not a rule? How broad should a framework be? How do you ensure that quality is maintained? How do you ensure that the team members adhere to the framework?

To begin with, a lot of frameworks are already set out in *laws* that apply to everyone. Take the law governing dismissal, for example. If a team member is not performing satisfactorily they can't just be fired; there needs to be a file stating things like what has been done to give the employee a chance to improve. That is the framework. The way in which the file is created, and what it looks like, are for the organization to determine. In a hierarchy the file requirements are often outlined in detail, but the question is whether this is necessary. We know from experience that a judge can be satisfied with an email exchange between the team and the non-performing team member, in which the agreements made and the way they have been evaluated are well expressed.

The Collective Bargaining Agreement also contains many frameworks that provide sufficient points of departure for teams to work with. Some agreements have stricter rules than others, but there is always room for interpretation by the organization.

So how do you develop a framework for the organization? Every organization needs to know things like whether they are providing good quality. A lot of systems and rules are developed to monitor this – but what would it look like if you put it into a framework, where various types of teams can use it in different ways? Both primary process and support teams could make agreements such as that the people for whom they work must be happy, and that they will do everything they can to prevent complaints. The teams could also agree on a way that they would know if their clients were happy. This method would then be discussed with the manager, who would ask about customer satisfaction on a regular basis (once a year is regular too ...). This obviously means that various methods would be developed, but would that be a problem? Each team comes up with its own method, so it will then also be keen to stick to it. The results are thus likely to be much better than when a central, locked-down system with which none of the teams can identify is poured out over the organization.

What you want is for team members to feel responsible for the quality of their work and not for operating a controllable system (with a mountain of paperwork as a result). That's the power of self-organization.

If the manager can – and dares to – look at frameworks in this way, then it's not too difficult to develop workable ones.

FRAMEWORKS AND RULES

We often see that the distinction between frameworks and rules is not always clear. A framework allows room for personal interpretation, and a rule doesn't offer this. Some examples of rules are:

- a team consists of 15 people;
- the team meets 1 x a month, for 1.5 hours;
- the report is written immediately after client contact and is recorded in the health care file;
- the employee is on site half an hour before starting work.

Some organizations set a fixed number of employees per team. This is used to determine how the teams are arranged, and to then distribute the teams across the regions or services. However, this is a format that is created from a managerial point of view and not from the actual content of the work. It sometimes happens – in some organizations that operate regionally – that a team consists of no more than six people, because there's no longer any work in the region concerned. In such a case, the team doesn't conform to the standard of fifteen people, so then another team of nine people from another region is added to it, to bring the total to fifteen team members. Phew, we conform to the rule ... However, in practice this proves to be unworkable, because the two teams have little in common. They will manage to find a way to make it workable, but the 'framework' is very much in their way here; it's not helpful.

When the situation *is* viewed from the point of view of the content, the framework could be formulated as follows:

'The team makeup should be such that all team members make a meaningful contribution to the team result, and that it's possible to make decisions by consensus via good mutual consultation.'

When looked at in this way it means that teams of six people are an option, but sometimes it's logical to have a team of twenty people.

If the team feels that it is too large to be able to conduct meaningful discussions, then it will look for ways to solve that problem. The team will then look for solutions that are in keeping with the content of the work. Otherwise other – unnecessary – problems will develop, which are obviously undesirable.

Rule	Framework
The team meets 1 x a month, for 1.5 hours.	Meeting frequency is determined by the team, and should be such that all team members are involved in decision-making and the team is able to respond to current events.
The report is written immediately after client contact and is recorded in the health care file.	Each client contact is reported in the health care file, to optimise handover.
The employee is on site half an hour before starting work.	The employee ensures that he has adequate time to prepare for the day's tasks or: Nothing! (Because you can assume that the employee will be prepared, and it's rather patronising to tell him to do it, as well as how it should be done.)
Absenteeism is not to exceed 3.5%.	Working conditions on the team should be such that wrongful absenteeism is avoided.
The team consists of 15 people.	The size of the team should be such that consultation and decision-making are easily achieved.

As these examples show, it's often possible to create a framework rather than a rule. This gives the team flexibility to interpret the subject at their discretion.

However, sometimes this is not possible or desirable. When setting productivity standards, the lower limit is a rule. The team is able to perform above the norm, but it's agreed with the team members that they will not perform *under* the norm.

Another example of a rule is: in unsafe situations, a team member has the right to carry out the task with a colleague.

FRAMEWORKS ARE SOMETHING YOU DEVELOP TOGETHER!

The success of a workable framework is also determined by the way in which the framework is developed. Many managers make frameworks *for* the teams, motivated by the needs of the organization and the manager (i.e. control). But in a self-organization, you want to develop things that are helpful for the team members as well as serving the organization's goal. This can only be achieved when managers and team members join each other at the table.

In a discussion about framework development, the manager and/or team members indicate what they need (with regard to a particular issue) in order to carry out their work properly. Requests for frameworks can therefore come from both sides.

Manager and team members discuss the possibilities together.

SETTLING ON FRAMEWORKS ON WHICH TEAM MEMBERS DISAGREE

Of course, sometimes the organization requests something that team members are opposed to. For example, there are sometimes issues relating to holidays and days off. In order to assure the organization's continuity, it may be important that employees don't take more than two weeks of holiday in summer, or the business may be closed for a certain period and the employees are compelled to take certain days off at that time (e.g. between Christmas and New Year).

The management naturally has reasons for these requests, and they can be discussed. Within the margins provided, the teams can determine how they will apply the rules within their team, but team members may not (for example) be permitted to take four weeks' consecutive holiday. That would mean that agency workers would need to be brought in to cover the absence, resulting in additional costs to the organization.

The team and the manager can discuss whether the frameworks are workable for the team involved. If there are reasons why the framework doesn't work for a particular team, the manager can choose to make an exception for that team.

The organization's continued existence is also important to self-organization. If the interests of the organization are not served, everyone will be out of a job. In a hierarchy the managers sort that out themselves, and in a self-organization the problems are solved together with the teams, meaning that the content of the work is more centrally placed. And all within the bounds of reason!

PROGRESS RATHER THAN MONITORING

Because the team members are responsible for the results, the manager no longer holds supervisory meetings, but progress meetings. These are used to discuss the way the team functions: whether the members are able to work according to the organization's vision, whether the frameworks are satisfactory, whether the desired qualitative and quantitative results can be achieved, and whether the collaboration is running smoothly.

Anomalies and any problems will be discussed, but these do not necessarily need to be resolved during that discussion. The question of whether the team members believe that there are sufficient possibilities for finding a solution can also be discussed. If there are too few options, the manager can ask what the team members need in order to move forward.

A pitfall for the manager here is that he may be tempted to solve any problems that may come up or may give the team assignments. This is often motivated by fear; previously he was responsible for the solution, and in the mindeset of, 'team members can't take on this responsibility, I should tell them what they have to do ...' he takes over too much of their task. Or he responds out of habit: if there's a problem, you tell people what they should do.

Besides making it impossible for the team to solve the problem themselves, this type of behaviour shows the team that the manager thinks they're not competent. If this happens regularly, the team will be increasingly reluctant to take the initiative to solve their problems. After all, the manager will do it – and do it better to boot (in their eyes, at least).

THE TEAM'S NOT KEEPING TO A FRAMEWORK. NOW WHAT?

At a certain point, the manager might see that a team is not keeping to the agreed frameworks. Obviously he talks to them about it. How does the discussion go? The manager begins by letting the team know how he views things and pointing out the way in which the team is operating outside the framework. At this point it's important that the manager makes it clear that he's interested in talking about it, and is curious about the reasons why it's happening.

He could start the discussion like this: 'I see that you're regularly getting complaints about the fact that you've failed to keep to your agreements with a number of clients. That doesn't meet the agreement that we made about "good quality", because that agreement says that it's important to stick to agreements made with clients. What are your thoughts on this?'

The team members will then explain how they are addressing the issue. If they already have a plan for preventing further complaints, they can present it. If the manager sees snags in it, he will discuss them with the team. The team members can then take this advice on board and continue with their plan. If there's no plan and the team members don't have any ideas about how to solve the problem, the manager can make it clear that he thinks that this is important, and ask what the team thinks they need in order to come up with solutions. The manager can then agree on a deadline on which he and the team will see whether the efforts have yielded the desired results. This allows the responsibility for implementation to stay with the team.

In extreme cases, the manager can state that the team must adhere to the framework and can agree on consequences if the team members still fail to do so.

In practice, however, when the manager conducts the discussion well, this is not often necessary.

MANAGER – TEAM COACH RELATIONSHIP

The manager and the team coach are two key staff members for the teams. Each of them assists the team in carrying out their duties. It's therefore very important that the two have a good relationship – not just so they can support the team, but also to shape the self-organization in the best possible way.

The coach is not in the line of hierarchy between the manager and the team; the coach is on the same level as the teams and the manager is above them.

A good relationship begins with respecting each other in these positions. However, we have often observed that the manager tends to place the coach in a hierarchical position between him and the team – as a new team leader, in fact. This positioning is reflected in statements such as:

'Coach, can you just check with the team that they're working on filling the vacancy?'

'Coach, the team members recently disagreed on ..., how was that solved?'

'Coach, I'd like you to talk to them about how they're dealing with ..., because something there really isn't working. I'd like to receive a report on it next week.'

'Coach, I know you're working on resolving the disagreement, but what are you actually doing about it? Is there any chance that you could speed it up a bit?'

'Coach, team X has a problem, how are we going to tackle it?'

In principle, the manager and the coach do not need to have contact about the team's progress. Contact from the manager to the team is a direct line, and if the manager thinks the team should make use of the coach, he can advise them to contact the coach. The team is responsible for consulting – or not consulting – the coach.

The manager also talks to the team members about the way in which the coach helps them. The team members obviously need to be happy with that; only then does the position prove its worth. If the team members are not happy, then the manager will inform the coach of this and subsequently encourage the coach and the team to talk to each other about the issue in order to improve their relationship.

Conversely, it may be that the team let the coach know that the manager – team relationship is not working well. The coach can then advise the team to discuss this with the manager.

MAKING DECISIONS

Even in self-managing organizations, there may come a time when the manager needs to make a decision – for example when a team member's performance is not up to standard, or if a team is unable to work within the organization's frameworks.

How does the manager deal with a team member whose performance is below expectations? The team regularly receive client complaints about their colleague Peter, and they discuss the issue with him. Agreements are made and Peter tries to improve. At the evaluation held after the agreed period, however, it is clear that the complaints have not reduced in number. The team members are finding it difficult to take the next step and they inform the manager. The manager advises the team to consult the coach, and perhaps also to request advice from the HR department. The team report on the situation during discussions with the coach, and it may eventually become clear that Peter is unable (or unwilling?) to change. The team indicate that they are no longer confident that there will be any improvement and they inform Peter that they will be handing the matter over to the manager with the request that Peter is dismissed from the team.

The manager examines the reports and decides whether enough has been done to justify this conclusion. He then makes a decision. This may mean that he requests that Peter be dismissed, but based on the precise situation he may also choose to see whether Peter would be better placed in another position within the organization. He might even weigh up whether – again depending on the situation – to order the team to put up with Peter as a team member.

However in our example, where Peter has been the cause of many complaints, this is not the most obvious choice.

Obviously the manager leaves the process of improvement completely up to the team and the team coach. He has faith that they will follow the process properly, and only acts if his help is required in order to enable them to move forward.

THE TEAM OF MANAGERS ON THE SAME PAGE

In a well-functioning self-organization, it's important that managers are all on the same page and that they facilitate their teams with the same principles as a starting point. That means they have regular contact about the way in which problems are resolved – and it goes without saying that when doing this, they use self-organizing principles. It's important for people to ask questions and alert each other when managerial and hierarchical ways of thinking pop up, including when it comes to the way the teams are treated.

Strange situations and dissatisfaction will result if one manager facilitates the teams and allows them plenty of leeway to work within the frameworks, while another assigns and monitors projects. Even when they work in different departments, team members are often in contact with each other and the organization's ongoing development towards self-management will stagnate.

How do team managers end up working based on different principles? Usually the management or Board of Directors makes the decision to change to self-organization. If this decision is made hastily (see also Chapter 2, on introducing self-management) and little time and energy is devoted to providing support, we see that the management level is precisely where discord can persist. With their particular view of people and work, some managers see many advantages to self-organization and are – by nature – already well along the path of facilitating the teams. Others see things differently, and want to hold on to control.

In our view, there is an important task for the directors here. They are in the position to make the call for the organization to change to self-management, while at the same time they are the ones who ensure that the process is well-designed and that everyone is on the same page.

If, after a number of discussions, it's clear that a manager (or managers) is unable to comply with self-organizing principles, and the directors are sticking with their decision to move to self-organization, then there's probably not a place for this manager in the organization going forward.

When the management tolerates employees thinking and acting in another manner, a clear conflict develops between managers when discussing problems in daily practice. Who's right? Those who say that the team members are perfectly able to cope with the responsibility, and that he will be there to help them if they have any problems (the manager facilitates self-organization)? Or those who say that in practice they don't see the team members stepping up to their responsibility and that as a result they still have to take care of a lot of issues for the teams (the teams *can't* step up to their responsibility because the manager doesn't give them the space to do so)?

They will never reach agreement because they disagree on the basic principle! If this situation arises and is not corrected, then in most cases it signals the beginning of the end of self-organization. This is largely because the managers who *do* want to apply self-management don't have the opportunity to put it into practice.

MANAGING USING PROCESS *AND* CONTENT, THE NEW ART OF MANAGEMENT

If the manager manages and doesn't facilitate, he can 'limit' himself to content in talks with the team members. But if he wants to facilitate then there's also another dimension, namely the process. He not only wants the team members to perform good work; he also wants them to take responsibility. That means that he has to look further than simply whether a problem has been solved or not. He will also need to discuss whether the team members *want* to solve the problem, whether they *can* solve it, and what they need in order to be able to do that.

During these discussions, he needs to connect engagement with the content ('What is the problem?') to the process side ('What are you going to do about it?').

If the group doesn't have a great deal of energy for finding solutions, this often manifests in resistance: 'It can't be solved, we've already tried this and we've tried that, now it's your turn ...' The manager can then reply, 'It's still your responsibility to find a solution. What might help you to get a bit closer to an answer?' He ignores the (unspoken) reproach and investigates whether and what opportunities there are, allowing the team to take responsibility.

Sometimes this takes some time and perseverance from the manager, but that patience is usually rewarded. If he addresses the problem directly, he will confirm the idea that the teams are not able to solve their own problems. Instead, he works on the assumption that they *can* do it, but perhaps need a bit of support to do so. He then follows up on the way that the team feels that he or another staff member can help them with it.

The manager thus shows that he takes the team members seriously in the fact that it's normal to not always immediately know how to solve something, and shows that he has confidence in the fact that they will manage it.

The result is self-confidence and a positive energy that stimulates creativity in the team members, so that problems suddenly become less serious and the team members do manage to arrive at a solution.

SOLUTION-ORIENTED MANAGEMENT

The way in which the manager communicates with the team members is solution-oriented, based on formulating their wishes and needs, and he uses the Solution Driven Method of Interaction (the SDMI®, which we discuss in Chapter 7).

He formulates objectives, asks what the team members think of them, discusses things with them on an equal footing, and makes agreements. He also continues to ask what the team members want to achieve and what they would like.

He communicates with them on an equal basis; he takes responsibility for his own tasks and leaves the team's responsibility to the team members. He doesn't take over anything. He also respects the differences between the team members; not everyone needs to be equally good at everything. Good is good enough, sometimes the 'stars' can take care of specific tasks with the consent of the other team members, and sometimes a colleague can compensate for things that another staff member isn't that good. The manager looks at the team result.

He also doesn't make an issue of the past; if an earlier agreement isn't working, then he looks at what is needed *now* in order to achieve the goal.

Working with the Solution Driven Method of Interaction® means that the manager and the team members work together to achieve goals, rather than making using complaints and nagging to make someone feel guilty, and constantly being engaged in a battle with them.

Above all, self-organization means shaping co-operation between the various levels and staff in the organization.

4
Support

However beautiful the strategy, you should occasionally look at the results.
– Sir Winston Churchill –

In a hierarchy, over the years staff members have had a a great deal of influence in developing and defining regulations, monitoring systems and policy development.

The developing of lots of regulatory and monitoring systems achieved uniformity and made it possible to control the primary process. The employees therefore experienced the staff as being an additional monitoring body, alongside the monitoring task already fulfilled by the manager.

Staff services do this in their own specific fields: human resources management, administration, communications, IT, legal affairs, public relations, and training.

In a self-organization, though, about the focus is not on the uniformity and control of the primary process, but on space, flexibility and self-discipline. So how can staff apply their valuable, specific knowledge and expertise? Doesn't this call for a different interpretation of the staff's duties?

STAFF SERVE THE LINE WORKERS

In both self-managing and hierarchical organizations, the supporting staff serve the line workers. Controlling systems and procedures is no longer the priority in a self-organization, so the staff can increasingly focus on supporting the line workers in terms of content, improving the quality of products and services, and developing tools that help the employees to feel supported in carrying out their duties. For example, this might include a registration system that is simple and easy to fill out while still providing the necessary information, meaning that employees have time left over to carry out their primary task.

In a self-managing organization, the staff can get back to the original objective: facilitating the line workers, and using their specialised skills to find solutions to problems the line workers encounter. These solutions need to be helpful for the team members. The teams in a self-organization make their own choices, so there will be differences between the teams. This also means that the staff tailor their advice to each team's specific situation. In practice this may mean that different teams receive different advice for something which at first glance appears to be the same problem. Of course, the varied advice given still needs to conform to the organizational frameworks, legislation and collective bargaining agreements.

In addition to coming up with solutions to problems, support departments will also consider the best way to provide the teams with information. The better and more accessible the information, the better the team members are able to carry out their duties. Here, too, it's important that the information system is tailored to the teams' needs and way it will be used; the IT department can develop a fabulous application, but if the team members have a lot of trouble finding the right information or if only one part of the application's capabilities are used, then unfortunately it's not a good application.

LETTING GO ...

When self-organization is introduced, the staff will need to say goodbye to certain tasks that they often really enjoyed doing. In a hierarchical setting, staff can indulge in developing policies and procedures, and they often don't worry too much about whether they can be executed. Complaints from those who do the work often have little effect.

When working in a self-managing organization, staff have to let go of the idea that they have responsibility for, and can therefore be held accountable for, the quality of the primary process. The line workers are responsible for this. The staff are responsible for the advice they give. This advice must be of assistance in carrying out the work in the primary process.

The proven formula E = Q x A shows how this works: the Effectiveness of advice is equal to the Quality multiplied by the Acceptance by the user.

For example, the safety adviser recommends fantastic safety clothing, with which the risk of burns is zero. The quality rating is a 9. But the wearer finds that she can hardly move in the clothes, which makes it almost impossible for her to do her job. The clothing's user doesn't give it a high acceptance figure, namely a 2. She is more likely to ignore the clothing than to put it on. The effectiveness of the measure is therefore not high: 9 (quality) x 2 (acceptance) = 18 (effectiveness of the advice). However, if the safety specialist recommends clothing which has a high comfort rating (quality an 8) and may provide less protection, but is nonetheless better than not wearing protective clothing and thus acceptance is significantly higher (7), then the effectiveness of the decision is 56. That's more than three times as high as the clothing that is qualitatively very good.

It is therefore important that the staff member concerned knows what's important to the team members when performing their work, so that he can come up with appropriate recommendations. He must let go of the idea that the qualitatively best solution is also the one that will work best in day-to-day use. Once staff members have experienced how grateful the team members can be for advice that is a perfect fit for their situation, any resistance they might have to their new role in the self-organization itself will melt away like snow in the sun.

STAFF – MANAGER RELATIONSHIP

The manager has final responsibility for the work the teams do, and thus also responsibility for developing the frameworks, policies and regulations within which they work. The supporting staff can develop frameworks and policy, but the manager (together with the teams) ultimately determines whether or not these will be applied in practice. The manager, not the staff member, is also responsible for proper implementation, even though the staff member is given responsibility for this in many hierarchical collaborations.

The manager can ask the support staff to develop something, and the team members can give the support staff more information on its use. The support staff will then advise the manager, who in turn makes a decision based on this advice.

The manager will hold discussions with the team members to discuss whether the policy frameworks and procedures provide adequate support for them to carry out their duties. If adjustments are needed, the manager will speak to the support staff again to determine a suitable adjustment based on their specialist knowledge and skills.

STAFF – TEAM RELATIONSHIP

When giving advice on the policy and frameworks to be developed, the staff member chiefly deals with the manager. He keeps on top of the situation in the teams and asks what would help the team members to, for example, be more efficient with schedules, or working with the intranet.

He then gets to work with this information, possibly checks with team members again to see whether they support his ideas, and presents a proposal to the manager. The manager then discusses the results with the team members.

The staff member can take the initiative to develop something, but needs to discuss it with the manager to get permission to take it to the teams. That contact, therefore, goes through the manager.

There is otherwise a danger that the teams will be inundated with requests from overzealous staff to talk to them about topics which the manager can already predict will not be relevant to them (at least at that time).

Team members, however, should always be able to call on staff for clarification of specific matters. These might be questions about the collective bargaining agreement, enforcement of the Sickness Benefit Act, dismissal rules, training questions, administrative matters, questions about marketing and PR and legal affairs. But the team members can also go to the staff for advice on the application and interpretation of laws or effective administrative procedures and IT applications.

If questions from team members appear to have consequences for already-developed frameworks (they are too broadly or too narrowly defined, so team members can't really use them), the staff member refers the team to the manager.

INFORM OR MOTIVATE

We have previously stated that the determining role that staff members have in a classic organization (whether or not they want to) also carries responsibility. They are sometimes addressed regarding (and held to account for) the fact that employees may or may not follow the agreed procedures. If new policies have to be implemented, this task is often delegated to staff. Because the staff are assigned this task, they also feel responsible for motivating and convincing employees. This can result in some confusing situations, because in the employees' eyes the manager is responsible. For teams, it feels like having two captains on one ship.

In a self-managing organization, the staff member may be limited to informing the team members of the new guidelines or procedures. After all, he has expertise in this area and was probably there at the cradle of the new directive, so if there are specific questions then he's the obvious person to answer them. If team members have strong objections and so don't agree with the directive, the staff member can refer them to the manager. And that's a relief! For staff, too, it is not always easy to feel responsible for something that should actually be on the manager's plate. We assume here that the manager also knows that he has this responsibility.

If the staff member is clear about his position within the self-organization, there may be initial disappointment due to the fact he has largely lost the freedom to develop things on his own initiative. On the plus side there's also satisfaction in the new scope of the job, because he is once again able to focus on the core tasks, namely: advising and informing others of practical applications in his field.

UNKNOWN, UNLOVED

Despite the supporting services being charged with an important task in both traditional and self-managing organizations, the employees who carry out the primary process are not always familiar with what they do. The staff's work is done largely behind the scenes, and as a rule employees see only the results. The way in which these results were achieved mostly stays hidden. This often leads to us/them thinking, which is something that can result in a gulf between staff and line workers even in self-organizations.

When teams begin to self-manage they are also expected to carry out organizational tasks, such as tasks in the areas of procurement, administration, finance and HR. In other words, in the staff services' territory.

Teams regularlyget started on their organizational tasks without thinking to ask the supporting services for help first, while the purpose of that support is precisely to facilitate the teams. Employees might spend many hours interpreting quality criteria, while a member of the quality control staff could let them know what it's all about in an hour-long presentation.

Employees from staff departments could avoid team members starting work unprepared by giving them more information on the background of their work, and the necessary (sometimes prescribed) procedures. This would obviously only cover those issues with which the team members are directly confronted – no more information than necessary! For example, when recording billable hours, the administration department could provide insight into why the recording method used is a good one, and what would happen if a team member made mistakes with it. This motivates team members to do the task properly, and motivates their colleagues address it with them if it's not done correctly.

The staff members may also be able to tell the team members more about how the staff can assist the team members with organizational tasks. This might then encourage the team members to ask for help more often, and more quickly. All this can eventually lead to more understanding of each other's work.

SERVICE CENTRE

Some organizations set up a service centre to enable communication between the teams and the supporting services to run more smoothly. The service centre is staffed by one or two employees who discuss the question with the team. The service centre staff member ensures that the question gets to the right specialist, and the specialist then answers the question or gets in touch with the team to discuss the issue in more detail.

This means that the team members don't have to go looking for the right person to help them, running the risk of being sent from pillar to post.

The establishment of a service centre is a particularly customer-friendly initiative for team members, giving them easy access to the staff.

TEAMS OF SPECIALISTS

Some organizations work with specialists who by law also bear a certain responsibility. Examples include medical and paramedical staff, psychologists, psychiatrists and remedial educationalists. We'll refer to them here as 'specialists'.

We are often asked where, and in which way, these staff should be placed in the organization to be most effective. There's no ready-made answer, because it depends on a lot of factors: the specific qualifications and competences, the nature of the work, the extent to which specialists need to be attached to a team, the way in which the rest of the organization is organized. In short, there are too many factors that make it difficult to give a ready-made answer.

Some organizations choose to place the specialists together in a single team, under the responsibility of the Director. The specialists have 'on call' contact with the team, depending on the problem for which specialist knowledge is requested. They function as a self-managing team, discuss the teams' questions and decide amongst themselves which of them is best placed to answer these questions.

Other organizations choose to attach the specialist to one or more teams for a set number of hours per week.

Obviously there are other options as well. Our advice is to use the principle of self-management to determine the most logical choice for each situation.

5
The team coach

Judging doesn't mean understanding.
– André Malraux –

The purpose of the team coach position is to support the team. The coach is there as and when needed to help the team members to develop skills, thus enabling them to shape their collaboration process.

Some organizations think that in the long term, the coach will no longer be necessary. They assume that a team goes through a number of phases (Tuckman) and is ultimately able to work so independently that no coach is needed. However, this would imply that the composition of the team remains the same, that the team members don't change, and that the environment in which the team works doesn't change either. Obviously this isn't true. Everything is constantly changing: team members resign and others replace them; at times team members are not feeling great in themselves and so have a particular (often negative) influence on the team; there are changes within the organization that the team members have to learn to cope with, etc. One minute everything might seem to be going well, and then a week later something happens that means that the team need the coach's help.

On the other hand, the team members might think that the team is functioning just fine, while the coach sees things that the team members can't see themselves and which might lead to conflicts down the track. The coach then needs to be able to discuss this with the team, on her own initiative.

For these reasons, we're in favour of the team always having a coach available to help them.

POSITION IN THE ORGANIZATION

There are various viewpoints on the coach's place in the organization. Some organizations choose to make the coach part of the supporting services, so the position is not part of the line. The coach then has no direct relationship with the manager of the teams she coaches, and the teams view the coach as being more independent.

However, the manager and the coach both have a direct relationship with the teams, each from a different angle: the manager facilitates the team from the line and has decision-making powers on matters that the team doesn't have the authority to decide on. The coach facilitates the team in terms of their teamwork.

The manager and coach talk regularly about what the teams need in order to perform their tasks well, although the coach doesn't share any specific team information. She talks in general terms about situations that are difficult to solve and preconditions that make it easier for the team to operate. The manager can support the coach in her role where needed, and ensures that the coach doesn't lead or manage the team. After all, that's the manager's task (from a distance). The managers make decisions about frameworks and the coach supports the teams, without pressuring them. In turn, the coach ensures that she doesn't act as an extension of the manager.

SHOULD THE COACH BE ATTACHED TO THE TEAM?

When setting up self-organizations, we are regularly asked which one is better: having a specific coach attached to a specific team, or a group of coaches who are available to the teams, which a team can approach as they see fit.

Our preference is for a coach who is attached to the team. The coach gets to know the team, and vice versa. It's then easier for the coach to spot changes in the team that may require her guidance. For example, she might see that one or more team members are dissatisfied with the situation within the team, but their concerns are being brushed aside by other team members. This can eventually lead to conflict. Team members see those changes too, but they often think that they'll just go away on their own – until they become too complex, and by then a conflict often already exists and it's harder to resolve the situation.

It's easier for team members to ask a coach for help when they know the coach. If they have a choice of coaches it becomes more difficult, because they don't have a good connection to the coach.

Working with a pool of coaches can mean that a team goes from one coach to another for help, and so don't manage to solve their problem. Some team members may also have an interest in the problem persisting, for example because they risk losing their dominant position in the team. If those team members start to feel cornered, they can blame the coach for not offering them effective help to solve the problem. They then turn to the next coach, and the process begins again. In this type of situation, it can take a long time to figure out what's preventing the team collaborating effectively.

Using an assigned team coach can prevent these types of situations, because the team doesn't have the option of switching to another coach. Their own coach is able to continuethe process of solving the problem, without interruption.

THE TEAM COACH'S TASKS

The coach's role can be described as *'supporter of the team'* – asked, but also unasked. If a team has questions about anything, they can always call on the coach for assistance. Sometimes the coach will have to refer them to someone else, but mostly she will be able to assist the team herself by asking questions, steering them towards ways of finding solutions, and giving advice. She supports the team as a group, but also supports the individual team members.

In principle, any and all subjects can be addressed during discussions with the coach. The coach focuses on supporting the team in the way the team members try to find solutions to the problems; she doesn't work on content-focused solutions.

The coach is also tasked with pointing things out (*signalling*), both to the team members and to management. She is often the first to see the impact of policy decisions at the team level. The management may think that it's a good idea to make each team's sales figures public, but the coach sees that this decision creates more competition between teams. The question is whether or not this is a desirable development. This is something that the coach can bring to the management's attention.

The coach works for multiple teams, and sometimes she sees a problem arise in multiple teams which could be centrally resolved within the organization (for example, the information system might not be functioning properly). At first she will advise the teams to discuss this with their manager, but if she is able to say that there are many teams with the same issue it's obvious that a solution is needed urgently.

She might also take the initiative to start the development of frameworks in the organization, or to change existing frameworks when teams signal that these frameworks don't seem to be very workable.

The same goes for developments relating to the self-managing organization. Self-management in an organization is constantly evolving, and the effects of centrally-made decisions are clearly visible in the teams. The coach can take initiatives for both staff and line workers to enable them to discuss these effects, for example dealing with absenteeism.

Another important task is *mediating and supporting when there are problems or conflicts*. Where people work together, sooner or later there will always be friction or conflict. Team members are usually involved to a greater or lesser extent, so it's not always easy for them to resolve these types of situations. In a hierarchy the manager usually solves the problem, but in a self-managing organization the responsibility lies with the team. A coach can help with this.

The coach is also responsible for assisting *individual employees* with solving work-related problems. Sometimes it's nice for a team member to discuss certain matters with the coach alone, because the problem is work-related but perhaps not directly team-related. But the team member might just want to have an 'outsider' as a sparring partner. The coach can then discuss the issue with the team member to determine how he can involve the team if that should prove necessary, or she can refer the team member to another person or group who can help him further.

The final – but not the least important – task is guiding the team members so that meetings are pleasant and effective. The team meeting is an important moment for a self-managing team. Team issues are discussed and decisions are made as a team. The coach can help to conduct the meetings so that everything runs smoothly.

SPAN OF COACHING

In a hierarchical organization, the *span of control* is a familiar concept: how many teams or employees can you monitor or manage? It obviously depends on the complexity of the work and the range of positions.

Could there be such a thing as a *span of coaching*? The 'coach of self-managing teams' position is a new one, so there is little or no research data available on the subject. However, experience shows that a coach should definitely not coach *too few* teams. That may sound strange, but if a coach has few teams and still wants to be 'useful' at work then she runs the risk of interfering with the teams too much. She will then be more inclined to give unsolicited 'help' with problems that the team would actually like to solve themselves. A team that is keen to take responsibility will very quickly find this coach intrusive. A team that's not inclined to take responsibility and gets along well with the coach will be more likely to hand the problems over to the coach to deal with.

In many organizations this rule of thumb is used for the span of coaching: an average of two hours per team, per week. When an organization first implements self-management, the average could be a bit higher: two to four hours per team per week. This includes individual contact, phone calls, answering emails and so on.

TEAM COACHING QUALITY CONTROL

Within the team, the team members are accountable to each other and if there are times when lower-quality work is delivered, they discuss this with each other. But how is the role of team coach assessed in a self-managing organization? How can the team coach's quality be monitored?

The team coach is directly under a manager or the director; that's the person to whom she reports. The manager can address the team coach regarding her performance at work. The teams keep the manager apprised of the coach's performance.

Sometimes the manager will be given unprompted information about the performance, either because a team is very satisfied with the coach's involvement, or because they have complaints. The manager then discusses these complaints with the coach so she can improve her performance.

Of course it may also be the case that the manager doesn't receive any unprompted information, or he wants to get a full picture of the coach's performance. Complaints and compliments obviously relate to specific incidents, and these don't give insight into the coach's performance across all her responsibilities.

The best way for the coach to get the full picture is to request information from the team members. He could get this information by periodically asking the team members to fill in a list in which they can give their opinion on their coach's work: does she offer sufficient and timely support, does she stimulate the team's self-managing skills, and if so how, is her advice helpful, does she respect the team's decisions, etc. The manager and the coach then discuss the results together, and can use them to help formulate a list of points for improvement.

Team coach evaluation
The following questions can be helpful in evaluating the team members' opinions of the coaching they have received.

The information should be processed anonymously, and the coach and manager can then discuss the results with each other.

1 Are you clear on the matters for which you can approach the team coach?

>>

>>

2 Does the team coach respond quickly enough to support requests?
3 Are you satisfied with the team coach's advice?
4 Is the team coach a good listener, does she show interest and does she ask questions?
5 Do you sometimes feel that the team coach takes sides in conflicts and differences of opinion between team members?
6 Does the team coach visit the team regularly to discuss issues that benefit or hinder the team's development?
7 Does the team coach provide sufficient assistance with procedures related to records, reporting and personnel matters?

SKILLS THE COACH NEEDS

Coaching self-managing teams requires specific skills and coaching techniques. These can generally be learned, but it's easier when the coach has a certain amount of talent. By 'talent', we mean certain innate qualities which we have observed are difficult to learn.

In order to be able to coach well, it's essential that the team coach has a *helicopter view*. In other words, she has to be able to *think in abstract terms*, able to *separate content and process* or *metacommunicate*.

When team members discussing an issue, the coach must be able to tell whether the team is working together constructively at the same time as she is listening to the content. If they are not working together well, she must be able to point out what might help to improve the co-operation or the discussion, without disrupting the discussion. For example, by saying, 'Lisa, do you see benefits as well as disadvantages? Or perhaps you have another suggestion?', you can give a team member guidance during the meeting without hurting his or her feelings.

A coach who can't metacommunicate looks at discussions at content level rather than looking at the way in which people are communicating, and tends to make assessments of the content.

Patience is another talent that the coach can help with by coaching well. It's important for the coach to keep to the pace set by the group. Sometimes a team needs time to make decisions, and it's not helpful to have a coach hounding them. The team members will feel the pressure and start to resist the coach, making the process counterproductive.

Finally, it's important for a coach to have an *unbiased interest in people*. A coach works with people, and all team members are entitled to have a coach who respects them as they are. This means that the coach treats all team members the same. A professional coach can set her own preferences aside and will treat all team members with sympathy and respect, so that they are always happy to approach her.

Coaches who naturally like to take the lead or who tend towards perfectionism will have to make more effort to help the teams to make their own decisions. They will be inclined to put their own stamp on the team, and even eventually to act as a team leader.

Coaches who tend to want to make other people happy will also face challenges with coaching. Their pitfall is that they are so focused on what the team wants that they don't ask the critical questions that could help the team to move forward.

TAKING SIDES: THE COACH'S OPINION

As mentioned earlier, the coach should not judge the content of the team discussions. The moment she does, she loses her neutral position and takes a 'side' in the discussion. She becomes part of the team, as it were, which is not her role; the coach should stand *alongside* the team. Judging doesn't have a major effect when dealing with issues on which the team members are more or less in agreement, ' but when there are disagreements, the team members will be quick to interpret this as being 'on X's side'. If this happens, neutral coaching is no longer an option as the 'losing' side doesn't feel comfortable with that coach any more.

However, there is an exception. When a team is looking for solutions to a problem and suggestions are made that are outside the organizational frameworks, the coach can comment. For example, in an organization where work is carried out 24/7, there might be an agreement that every team member must be available for all shifts. If David refuses to work on the weekends, or continually manipulates the scheduling to ensure that he isn't assigned to weekend shifts, the other team members may get annoyed. At a certain point the coach could remark, 'David, what you're doing, only working day shifts, is not in keeping with the frameworks. Your colleagues would like you to follow the rules. Would you like to do that?'

The coach gives her opinion of David's attitude, but by making reference to a framework or rule she stays impartial. After commenting, she immediately encourages team members to continue the discussion amongst themselves. By comparing the attitude to the framework she also shows how a potential conflict situation can sometimes be defused. This serves as an example for the team members to follow.

INTERVENTION TECHNIQUES FOR THE COACH

The art of coaching is being able to use the right intervention at the right time, thus helping the team members to move forward. We think that a solution-oriented coaching style is the best fit for a self-managing organization. The SDMI®, the Solution Driven Method of Interaction, is explained in more detail in the following chapter.

Short, clear interventions in line with what the team is working on, and that provide the least disruption to the team process, achieve the greatest effect. Detailed process descriptions and explanations about phases the team is passing through may lead to insight, but they can also bring the team to a standstill. They don't always lead to solutions. The same is true of objectives that coaches sometime pursue, such as strengthening the team members (strengthening them in what, and at whose request?) and providing insight into team members' qualities. Often these are actions that are not directly connected to the team members' needs, and the coach loses the connection with the team. When the coach immediately picks up on what's being said in the team then she keeps the connection, and the team members feel that her contribution has added value.

The team members will consult a coach when they feel like they're stuck in their way of co-operating, or when decision-making comes to a standstill. The coach aims to bring 'movement' to these processes with her contribution. For example, a standstill occurs when the team members continually communicate in generalities: 'We're not getting anywhere with decision-making', or 'It's quite difficult to talk to each other', and 'Things would go a lot better if everyone would just say what they mean'. The coach can make this vague language concrete by continuing to ask questions, such as 'What needs to happen before decisions *can* be made?' and 'Who needs to explain what they mean?' The box below gives some examples of how to make general statements concrete. This relatively simple intervention can enable a coach to move the discussion forward very quickly.

Chapter 9 gives an example of how the coach can use solution-focused questions to support the team process.

Vague comment from team member	Coach's reaction
'You can't please everyone.'	'Who can't you please?' 'What do they want that's different to what you want?'
'We need a leader again.'	'Why?' 'What does the leader have to lead then?' 'What's not being done that she would have to deal with?'
'That type of idea doesn't really belong here.'	'Which idea do you think doesn't belong here?' 'Why do you think that idea doesn't really belong?'
'It's not always easy to work on this team.'	'What do you find difficult?' 'What would you like to change?'
'I just have to let it sink in a bit.'	'How long do you need, so that we know when we can move on?'
'This team needs to talk about communication.'	'What should that sort of discussion aim to achieve?'

SOLICITED AND UNSOLICITED ADVICE

At certain points the coach may choose to give the team members solicited or unsolicited advice. Some coach training recommends that coaches don't offer advice. It's assumed that the coach's advice imposes a particular direction on the team and leaves the team members feeling that they're not free to choose their own path. In addition, a solution presented by someone else 'isn't as effective as one that you've come up with yourself.

However, we would assume that team members get their information from all over the place and get ideas from all sorts of media and people, so why not from a discussion with the coach?

What's important is what the coach does *after* she has given the advice. Does she then ensure that the team members use her advice as inspiration, or will she really 'sell' her advice to them? 'Selling' the advice forces a decision that the team members probably don't support. But the coach can also use her advice to draw attention to a different line of reasoning, stimulating the team members to think outside their usual paths. By allowing the team members to weigh up her advice, she stimulates them to form their own opinions. It's not a problem for the coach if her idea is rejected, because her aim is to simulate 'movement' in the team process and she looks at what her intervention 'stirs up'.

Sometimes the team members appear to accept the advice without question. When this happens, the coach will ask further questions about the arguments. For example if the team members say, 'If you say so, then it's fine', it's not an argument that demonstrates that they've thought the idea through properly. There is then a good chance that implementing the idea won't have the desired effect. The coach can also say, 'That doesn't sound like a good reason to take my advice. The intention is that you should all work on it, so why would this idea be a good solution for this problem?'

As a rule, giving advice usually works better than using leading questions to encourage the team members to formulate what you actually want to say. That's not as clear and direct, and the team members quickly realize that you are thinking in a certain direction. You could even say that it's a bit patronizing, as if the team members wouldn't be able to assess an idea fairly if they heard it from someone else.

INDIVIDUAL APPROACH

The individual approach is a technique which can enable the coach to effect a lot of movement in the team. We're used to seeing the team as a whole: 'The team has a conflict', 'The team's having trouble reaching consensus', 'Team X is such a great team!', 'There's so much gossip in Team Y'.

This can make it difficult for the coach to stage effective interventions. She might constantly address the team as a whole: 'You asked me to talk to you because you having so much gossip in your team is causing problems. I doubt that it's good for the team spirit, so how will you solve it?' The question is: who feels like she's actually talking to them personally? In practice we see that a general discussion about gossiping usually follows. Is it allowed, or not? When is it allowed? Or is it never allowed? ...

But what we want is for the team members to talk to each other about gossiping. That's also where the solution lies: in our eyes, the team is not a single unit that can be addressed as such. It consists of individuals, each of whom influences the team process in his or her own way.

Coaches who use the solution-oriented approach will address the team like this: 'Some of you have indicated that it's a problem for you that a few colleagues regularly say bad things about other colleagues. Who's got a suggestion for putting an end to this?'

When guiding discussions, too, the coach can use the individual approach to help the team members to feel that they are being personally addressed and encourage them to take their share of the responsibility. The box below gives a few examples.

Group approach	Individual approach
'Come on people, let's keep on track.'	'Lucia, what do you think of David's idea?'
'How are you going to take this up with each other?'	'Who's got a suggestion for a plan?'
'Perhaps in future everyone needs to keep a closer eye on their timekeeping.'	'Marian, Lucia would like to know if you will also meet the deadline next time? Could you do that?'
'This group is currently exhibiting survival behaviour; let's take a look at what's causing that.'	'Who has a suggestion for helping everyone to feel more comfortable on this team?'

EXERCISING INFLUENCE AND LONG-TERM EFFECT

There are times when the coach leaves a team and wonders what contribution she has made to, for example, improving their teamwork. The group might have talked about it a lot, but she doesn't really feel like much will change. When she goes back to the team a week later, the atmosphere is visibly less tense than the last meeting. Jokes are being made again, and the team members who were avoiding each other are now consulting each other about a shared problem. When she asks how collaboration is going, she's told: 'Your comment last time really got me thinking about how people respond to stressful situations differently. I suddenly realised that I'm really bad at prescribing how others should respond. So I've decided that I just won't make an issue out of it any more.'

Coaches exercise influence with *all* their interventions; it's just that sometimes the effects of their comments only become clear after some time has passed. Team members need time to process things; time to talk things over with each other again, or with their partners at home. A single comment from the coach can have a big effect in terms of improving how the team functions.

ENSURE GOOD POWER DISTRIBUTION

One pitfall that coaches should look out for is unequal power distribution. When discussing a problem, team members may place responsibility for the problem somewhere other than themselves, or simply not make any effort to solve it. The coach can respond to this by encouraging the team members to take responsibility after all: 'If you respond differently, you'll find that the client is more positive too', or, 'Really, if you'd put in more effort, you'd find that you *can* manage it.' The coach is clearly putting more energy into solving the problem than the team member is, and this puts pressure on the team member. The result is that a team member who feels cornered will then be less motivated to work on a solution. A conflict then develops between the coach and the team member, about something that wasn't actually necessary in the first place.

The team member is responsible for solving the problem. If he doesn't want to make the effort, then the coach should address it. If the team member says, 'Whatever I do, it doesn't achieve anything', then the coach can respond, 'Then I wouldn't do anything else if I were you.'

The reverse also occurs: the team wants to put lots of effort into solving a problem; the coach is beset by team members, people want to make lots of appointments with her to get her advice, and the team hangs on her every word. Probably the coach's first impulsive reaction is to try to back out of the claim that the team is making on her. However, chances are high that this will make them chase her even harder. It's better to have a discussion with the team members about their expectations.

THE MANAGER'S NOT DOING A GOOD JOB!

If the team members complain to you about their manager, this may cause a difficult situation for you as a coach. Perhaps the manager doesn't keep the team up to date, doesn't keep to his agreements, is regularly not contactable, and draws up frameworks that the team members can't work with.

The coach's first reaction might be, 'Oh, that's no good, something has to be done about it!' and she rushes to the manager, full of indignation. 'You can't treat the teams like that!'

What the coach is doing in this case is placing herself above the manager, as if she was his boss. The manager is obviously not going to be happy about that, and he will go on the defensive. This can seriously impact the coach/manager relationship.

With the team, too, the coach is placing herself in a position to which she has no right. She takes the responsibility away from the team, signalling to the team that they can't solve the problem themselves.

The conflict is actually between the team members and the manager, although the coach may be able to help the team to approach it. For example, the coach could stimulate the team members to discuss the issue with the manager in order to consider solutions. This allows the team to take responsibility. Such an approach preserves the individual coach/manager and coach/team relationships.

CONNECTION TO THE TEAM

The coach is responsible for ensuring that she has a good connection with the team; the good relationship between the team and the coach must be obvious. All team members should feel that the coach respects and listens to them. This is one of the reasons why coaches should not judge team members' opinions. If coaches do make judgements, they run the risk of looking into who's actually right and then – worse still – speaking to the team about it. When this happens, team members who have been told that they're wrong naturally don't feel that the coach respects them. When it comes to interpersonal problems it's almost impossible to determine who's right. Is it the one who doesn't stick to the agreements? Or the one who makes appointments without involving their colleagues, with the result that the others don't feel responsible for the appointments? Or is the team member who made the appointments without involving the colleagues actually the one who's in the right, because they almost never attend the meetings anyway?

If the coach in the middle makes no comment about who's right and who's wrong, and focuses her attention on ways that the team members can help to resolve the difference of opinion, she maintains a connection with all of the team members.

6
The self-managing team

The strength of the team is each individual member.
The strength of each member is the team.
– Phil Jackson –

How does self-organization operate within the team? How can team members collaborate and communicate in a way that allows them to meet their objectives in a fun and efficient way? And what else is needed in addition to good communication?

As we've already explained, the roles of the manager, the coach and the supporting staff are to facilitate the team, but that doesn't mean that the team members themselves don't have to do anything. A lot is expected from them, and self-organization calls for different knowledge and skills than working in a hierarchy does. Incidentally, and contrary to what some managers believe, most team members enjoy developing these skills and being responsible for the good functioning of the team. Self-organization generally gives the team members a lot of freedom to perform their jobs properly, and it turns out that level is not really important. Someone who works in 'cleaning' wants to approach his work professionally too, and to deliver a good result, just the same as someone who has a nursing degree or drives a truck. And all of them are able to handle – and to shape – responsibility in a self-organization.

In this chapter we will give some suggestions for working as part of a self-managing team.

PUTTING THE TEAM TOGETHER

We'll start at the beginning: putting a team together. When an organization decides to move to self-management, many managers think that they need to decide who will be working on which team. It's better to leave this decision to the team. They will determine whether the team makeup is well suited to the product, service or client.

For this reason, it's definitely a good idea to define frameworks for a team – capacities, degree of flexibility and so on – but once this is done the team members should be able to choose each other. The point at which the organization 'tips' to self-managing is a good time to give team members the opportunity to work as part of a team in which they feel at home.

In a hierarchy, team members' affinity for each other plays less of a role (although even here it's not unimportant), because there are individual job responsibilities. If problems develop, the manager or team leader solves them. In a self-managing team, the members have joint responsibility for the team result and therefore need to work things out together. If team members have a good affinity for each other, it will be easier for them to solve any teamwork problems.

For this reason, it's also important that the team members themselves are able to choose new colleagues to join their existing team. When this happens, we have seen that team members look critically at the qualities that team members already possess, which qualities they lack, and what they are therefore looking for in the candidate.

WHEN IS A SELF-MANAGING TEAM SUITABLE?

It's only once problems arise that you can see whether the team members are able to co-operate to solve them. When some team members are not very skilled in collaboration, every problem seems to end up in a team crisis. This leads to the question of whether certain requirements could be made of employees working in self-directed teams. We see that certain qualities are useful, and others can get in the way of teamwork.

The effectiveness of a self-managing team is partly determined by the degree to which the team members can form workable agreements with each other. Team members who are prepared to change their point of view to that of a colleague, and who are *creative* in forming *compromises* that all team members are happy with, will find it easy to co-operate. *Being prepared to 'give in' or compromise* is an attitude that shows that you're keen to co-operate and to take your colleagues into account. This has a stimulating effect, even when the team members don't immediately agree with each other. Compromise then usually follows.

In a self-managing team, colleagues should also jointly monitor the quality of the work they do. *'Resilience'* is a quality that is very useful here. When you speak to a colleague about something to do with the work, it has a positive effect if he doesn't feel that he's being attacked, but is instead prepared to take a look at the way he acts and to make adjustments. This then makes it easy to say something again the next time.

Respect for people who disagree is also a helpful quality. Team members who condemn 'dissenters' quickly create a tense atmosphere within the team. People who hold tight to their own opinions and place their values and norms above those of their colleagues, the *'bosses'* in the team, tend to drive the team members further apart rather than bring them together.

It's also difficult to hold discussions and make agreements with team members who are not solution-oriented and who tend to come up with one objection after another. These seekers of *'dragons on the path'* mean that making decisions is sometimes difficult or impossible, to the great irritation of their colleagues.

The last character we'd like to mention is the *busybody*. This is someone who finds it difficult to be flexible and tries to force the team to agree on a new rule for every exception that comes up. These team members can bring others to despair, because all the rules make it even more difficult for the others to find creative solutions to situations – and that is precisely one of the great advantages of working in a self-organization.

CO-OPERATION CONTRACT

Over time we see that each team develops its own culture, with its own agreements, tailored to the team members and the team's specific area of work. New team members usually respect the existing agreements. They settle in to the new situation, and only begin to join in the discussions about changes and making new agreements after a period of time has passed.

However, some new team members try to make their mark on the team very quickly, and want to bring existing agreements up for discussion as quickly as possible. These might be, for example, agreements on holiday planning and days off, and how team tasks are distributed. The 'older' team members then need to make an effort to enable the newcomer to adapt to the existing agreement culture.

These types of discussions can be avoided by including a clause in the contract stating that the new employee is aware of the current team agreements, and endorses them.

The team is advised to set out the team agreements in a so-called 'team handbook', which records all agreements by topic. Many teams record the agreements in the minutes or resolution lists, but it's difficult to refer back to these.

TASKS AND NO TEAM ROLES

In a self-managing team, the intention is that the team members bear joint responsibility for the results. Certain organizational tasks must be carried out to make that possible. In a hierarchy the team leader usually takes care of these tasks, but in a self-organization the team members do them themselves. These tasks are things such as scheduling and drawing up rosters, quality monitoring, improving working methods, maintaining external contacts, preparing for meetings, chairing and taking minutes, hiring new team members, etc. The activities that need to be done are also related to the team's area of work.

We call the activities 'team tasks'. The team tasks are periodically distributed among the team members who say they can do them or want to learn. Taking on a team task creates a greater sense of team responsibility in the team member concerned. Other than that, the team as a whole is still responsible for carrying out the team tasks.

We sometimes see that organizations turn work activities into roles: the planner, the chair, the HR role, monitoring results and finances. Each role usually involves a cluster of activities. The danger is that a role will be seen as a position in the team, which can bring a certain authority with it. This is definitely not how it should be. Sometimes we even see team members wanting to be paid extra because they've been performing the 'role' for so long.

The team members are all equal, and all have an equal say on all issues concerning the team. For this reason, we prefer to talk about team tasks rather than roles. Large team tasks can sometimes be divided into sub-tasks, meaning that multiple colleagues can take responsibility for an individual task. Examples include supervising interns or maintaining external contacts. Dividing tasks into sub-tasks allows team members with smaller contracts to take part in carrying out the team tasks. The person who performs the task does it for the other team members, and is therefore accountable to his colleagues. If the task is not carried out according to requirements, his colleagues can then ask him to account for this. When someone doesn't perform a team task very well, the task can be taken over by another team member.

TASK ROTATION

The team tasks should also be rotated amongst the team members on a regular basis, giving every team member the opportunity to carry out the team tasks. Carrying out team tasks is also a way to broaden your personal development. In addition, carrying out these tasks gives you a good picture of the team dynamics. This in turn creates a better understanding of the difficulties colleagues face. If you've also had to deal with a moody referrer, it makes it easier for you to empathize when your colleagues want to discuss this type of a problem with the team.

Team tasks can be rotated, say, twice a year – but not, as some teams do, once every three years. After that length of time a task has usually already become a 'position'.

New team members usually don't join the team task rotation until they know how the team works, so that they can make a useful contribution.

QUALITY ASSURANCE

Monitoring the quality of the work is a team responsibility in self-organizations. The manager sets the quality frameworks, and the team ensures and guarantees that the work is of good quality. The team members generally enjoy delivering good quality (after all, there was a reason they studied for a profession), and within self-organizations we make the assumption that professionals want to perform their work well. Team members have a direct interest in delivering good quality; the lines of communication with clients are short, and it's much more pleasant to get compliments for what you do than to get complaints.

There are various ways in which team members can monitor the quality of the work, and there's absolutely no need to create complicated, time-consuming systems for this. It's important that the team members know what's expected of them. The organization can facilitate the teams by using questionnaires to bring concrete form to the discussion about quality. Some easy-to-implement ways of monitoring and improving quality are discussed below.

Critiquing based on the desired results

It's difficult for team members to address each other directly about agreements that haven't been kept to or work that hasn't been carried out properly. People are scared of getting an aggressive response, which isn't so surprising – many people can't handle criticism, and they get angry. This is why critical messages should be partnered with positive comments: 'You're obviously very good at your job, but if you're in the position of having to have a difficult discussion again, you could try ...' Someone who really can't cope with criticism then usually only hears 'You're very good at your job', and doesn't get the underlying message at all, so there's no question of 'being held accountable for quality'.

Another way of saying something without receiving an angry comment in return is to ask questions to enable the other person to tell you about what's not going well: 'How did that conversation with ... go?', 'And how did she respond to ...?', 'Do you think you could have avoided that?', 'What have you learned for next time?' The colleague will probably feel patronized by this, and will be on his guard next time. With this approach, too, the effect on the quality will be zero due to its patronizing nature.

Our advice would be to express criticism as a wish: 'In the discussion with ..., which is quite a difficult one, would you be able to take her personal situation into account a bit more? She approached me about it later, and she found the discussion with you very difficult. You don't have to agree, but you do really make your colleagues aware of it, and then there's only one way to interpret the message'.

It is easier for people to respond to a request for change (a wish) than to a suggestion or a reproach.

'You realise that you waste a lot of time if you do things in this order?' (reproach)

then becomes:

'I think it would save you time if you do this first, and then that. What do you think?'

Asking for regular feedback is also something to consider. It shows that you are open to hearing criticism, which makes it easier for others to let you know what they think could be done differently.

Customer feedback

The consumer is an important source of information about the quality of the work. Everyone has consumers: the customer who buys your product, the client to whom you provide a service, the student to whom you provide education, the colleague for whom you do scheduling, the team member for whom you carry out the administration, and the colleague whose work you facilitate.

Unnoticed, they give you lots of information about the way you work. If you hear, 'I'm getting sent from pillar to post ...', then it's probably not clear who does what in the department. This is sufficient reason to hold a progress meeting.

The same is true when someone comments that the lesson wasn't as inspiring as last week's: 'It was *so* theoretical'. You could then consider making lessons a bit more practical, rather than simply thinking, 'The students always have to have something to complain about'.

We would like to add that large-scale customer satisfaction surveys are less effective, because the results can usually not be attributed to specific activities carried out by a team. It's better to allow those who work directly with the customer to research customer satisfaction. The team will take criticism from their own clients more seriously, because they have a connection to them and thus feel more responsible for the quality.

Shadowing a colleague

When people have been in a job for a period of time, they develop a way of working that feels comfortable for them. This often goes hand in hand with a restricted view of their own way of working, the so-called 'blind spot'. To reduce this blind spot, you might find it inspiring to spend a day shadowing a colleague and make a critical comparison of your respective working methods. Why does she do things that way? What different responses do you see from clients? How can you use these insights to make your own work even better and more interesting?

Intervision

Intervision is another way of broadening your horizons. In a discussion with your colleagues, you explain a situation to them for which you can't find a solution, or in which you think you should be able to do things better. They then ask you questions about that situation and give you advice on ways you could approach it. Your colleagues do this from their own perspectives, giving you a range of ideas about other ways of working.

In some organizations, intervision is obligatory: each team holds an intervision session every four to six weeks. The disadvantage of this type of ongoing commitment is that you end up talking to each other about it because you have to, not because you need to. Just as with the quality improvement methods, the same is true here: hold intervision meetings when they are necessary and relevant. When someone needs to have an intervision meeting with the other team members, they can raise the topic at – for example – the regular team meeting.

Appraisal interviews

What's sometimes true of intervision is especially true of performance appraisals (or assessment interviews or annual reviews): in most hierarchical organizations these are an institution, decked out with extensive policy systems, forms, interview techniques, training and just about everything else. Appraisal interviews were originally intended to be a two-way conversation between the manager and the employee about the employee's performance. This was in contrast to the assessment interview, in which only the manager's opinion was considered important (therefore very hierarchical). Agreements, including agreements on how the employee wanted to develop further, were set down during the appraisal interviews. The employee needed to accept the agreements, and otherwise he could appeal. At that time, the 1970s and '80s, it was revolutionary. To this day appraisal interviews are carried out faithfully each year, even when employees have been working to everyone's complete satisfaction for years, and both the employee and the manager find the discussion completely unnecessary.

At a certain point, organizations that want to change to a self-organization face the question: 'What about appraisal interviews?', because there is no direct manager to conduct the discussions. The director certainly doesn't have time to hold what may be up to 500 discussions per year.

Our answer: appraisal interviews are conducted within the team, because the team members are jointly responsible for their quality and development, and only when necessary. In practice this means that team members often choose a way of improving the quality of the work that is less time-consuming than an appraisal interview, but nonetheless has the same result, or they may choose to discuss the overall performance with one or two colleagues. The positive points and areas for improvement can also be discussed within the team by using the job description to exchange two 'tops' (things someone is good at) and two 'tips' (things that could be improved) with each other. If all team members do this for each other, this gives a fairly clear picture of their strengths and weaknesses.

Developing a uniform system of appraisal interviews is therefore unnecessary in a self-managing organization.

Team evaluation

In contrast to appraisal interviews, which are designed to map individual performance, the team evaluation aims to provide insight into the way in which the team members work together. Good teamwork is essential in a self-managing team, and if minor irritations and disagreements aren't discussed soon enough, they can grow into problematic conflicts which are much more difficult to deal with.

In a team evaluation, the team members examine the team functioning together and agree on possible improvements. The box below gives an example of a questionnaire that may be useful for structuring the discussion. The questions also state the criteria for a well-functioning self-managing team.

It can be a good idea to involve the team coach in the team evaluation. She can lead the discussion, enabling the team members to concentrate on the content.

Team evaluation

1 Is the team composition such that
   a personality differences are accepted?
   b differences around flexible deployment are accepted?
   c all professional and organizational tasks can be carried out?

>>

>>

2 Is there a 'willingness' to give in? In other words, are the team members able to modify or change their own opinions, with the aim of reaching agreement?
3 Is there agreement on the division of labour?
4 Are the team tasks assigned in a way that allows everyone to make sufficient use of each other's qualities?
5 Can people approach each other about the quality of the work?
6 Does the team possess sufficient knowledge to be able to support each other in professional terms?
7 Is the team able to, and does it have the tools to, tailor the demand for care/support to the available hours of work?
8 Are team members able to take a solution-oriented approach to problems?
9 Are decisions made by consensus?
10 Does the whole team bear final responsibility for all tasks that are carried out by the team?
11 Do all the team members look after each other?
12 Are the team members willing to help each other?

THE TEAM MEETING

The team meeting is an important part of the team process. If the team members have to produce a joint result, it's essential that they meet regularly to discuss it. The team meeting is where decisions are made, and given that all members of the team bear individual responsibility for the whole, everyone needs to attend.

A lot of people really dislike meetings, because they often have no structure and fail to produce results. Conversely, sometimes they are far too rigidly structured meaning that nobody feels free to discuss things, it's far too tedious, and the meeting is dominated by just a few colleagues. In a hierarchical situation, the manager usually talks for a large part of the meeting time, with announcements and agenda items that he finds important. Then he complains about the small contribution the employees make. And we don't think it's strange ...

Chapter 8 discusses the meeting model based on the Solution Driven Method of Interaction (see Chapter 7) in detail. Solution-oriented meetings are an important part of self-organization, because they are an efficient way of reaching broad-based decisions. A meeting model should also be easy to apply, so that the structure serves the content rather than the other way around.

In this section we will look at how team meetings can be structured.

Frequency

How often do meetings need to be held? Some organizations 'give' a team two hours of meeting time every four weeks. This is insufficient in most cases. It may have been enough in a hierarchy, but in that model the manager makes a lot of decisions without discussing them with the team members. In a self-organization the team members need to consult each other, and if there's not enough joint meeting time available then we soon see that the team members with big contracts end up making decisions about the daily routine. This eventually leads to a new hierarchy within the team, with (usually unintentionally) the people who work a lot having the most say.

The team members decide for themselves how much discussion time will be needed, and what's possible given the time that people have available. This also depends on the area of work.

The agenda

In a self-managing team, every team member has the opportunity to submit agenda items. Items will only be postponed (because the agenda for the meeting concerned is already too long), or even removed, if the submitter agrees.

In a traditional organization people are used to the manager making the agenda, and they comply with the management's decision – even if it means that their item is removed from the list because it is considered unimportant. Some self-managing teams retain this habit, and the chair takes over the manager's role and determines the agenda for the others. This gives one team member more say than the others, which is not the intention.

The tentative agenda is only finalised during the meeting. If there are more items than can be covered in the meeting time, the urgency of these is discussed and the submitter decides whether he thinks there is sufficient reason for his item to be postponed. Suggestions that affect every attendee (for example extending the duration of the meeting), however, are decided jointly. On paper this seems like a laborious process, but experience shows that team members are able to work through it quickly.

The chair

The chairship of a self-managing team can be viewed as one of the team tasks that each team member can perform; in a hierarchy the manager usually performs this task. The chair therefore has no additional powers. Some team members think this is a shame, and derive a certain status from this task which also allows them to claim more of a say. In most cases this results in conflict, because the other team members don't accept this. The task should be rotated regularly in order to prevent such problems.

In principle every team member can take on the task of chair, but for the sake of the quality of work in the team it's better to have the task performed by someone who has already mastered it reasonably well, or would like to learn. Poor chairship can cause too many problems for the team. Incidentally, this applies to all tasks; a poor planner also causes a lot of misery for a team.

DECISIONS BY CONSENSUS

One of the consequences of working in a self-organization is that the teams make their decisions by consensus (everyone agrees with the proposed decision, or indicates that they have no objection). Responsibility for the team results rests with the team and in order to be able to take that responsibility as an individual team member, employees need to have decision-making authority. This applies to all team members, and it follows from there that the decisions are made together and all team members agree. This doesn't mean that everyone always has to agree wholeheartedly with everything. In practice that often leads to endless discussions without a workable result.

What we mean is that the team members work together to look for workable solutions to problems in the team, and that objections are inverted to become proposals. What you often see during discussions is that objections become reasons to reject a proposal and thus the proposal is set aside. Decision-making then stagnates as a result. Team members should be asked to come up with proposals for solving the objections, thus bringing the team members' views closer and making it easier to reach jointly supported decisions. This creates an optimistic atmosphere in which teamwork is enjoyable.

MINUTES, RESOLUTIONS, TEAM HANDBOOK

It's obviously a good idea to record the agreements made during a meeting, so everyone has access to the same information and there's no room for interpretation. The same rule applies here: don't do any more than necessary.

Many teams automatically draw up a very detailed record of how the discussions progressed. Sometimes it looks like a play:

John: ...

James: ...

Elizabeth: ...

The minutes are then put in a cupboard and no-one ever looks at them again. Diving into those thick folders to find a discussion again to see what agreements were made is far too daunting.

What's actually required in order to work is a good, simple wording of the decisions. If a team member needs to take action on something, then simply noting 'who', 'what to do' and 'by when' is sufficient. Both the decisions agreed and the actions to be taken can be recorded in the 'decision and action list'. If it's important for absent team members to know how a discussion played out, then a brief mention can be made of the proposals and arguments covered. This saves a great deal of time.

It's more efficient to archive the decisions and agreements according to topic. For example, all agreements related to drawing up the roster will be collated and filed under the heading 'rosters'. If an agreement is changed, the old agreement is discarded and the new one is filed in its place. If this is done consistently (someone could take responsibility for this team task), then a so-called team handbook (paper or digital) is created which contains all relevant team agreements. New team members can read this to find out how things work in the team and can settle in quickly.

Doing things in this way means that the team doesn't waste precious time on creating detailed minutes that no-one reads, but there is still a good overview of the decisions, which makes it easier to keep each other accountable for these agreements.

TO EMAIL OR NOT TO EMAIL

We'd like to take a brief look at how email is used. These days everyone communicates via email, WhatsApp and the like. There's nothing wrong with that – it saves time, you don't have to wait until someone has time to talk to you, and it's cheap.

However, some team members clearly find email a comfortable medium when there are irritations. It seems easier to say what's bothering you if you don't have to say it to your colleague's face – you write it in an email and that will get the message across.

But this is a misapprehension. The irritation almost always comes through in the writing, and words on paper seem harder, more direct and more emotional, because the extra dimension of face-to-face contact (or your voice, if you're talking to someone on the phone) is missing. In addition, not everyone is able to set their thoughts down on paper in a way that conveys their point exactly as intended. Situations can thus escalate unnecessarily.

It's a better idea to discuss irritations in person with the colleague concerned. If that really doesn't work, then it might be wise to ask someone else to read the email first so you can be sure that your (hopefully) good intentions come across.

The reverse also applies: if you receive an unpleasant mail from a colleague, don't answer immediately while you're all riled up, but leave it for at least a day or speak to your colleague in person.

WORKING ON A MULTIDISCIPLINARY TEAM

In a multidisciplinary, self-organizing team, colleagues from different fields are jointly responsible for the team result. This is a common team composition in the health care sector. There are also examples of multidisciplinary teams in education (different subject teachers teaching a group of students) and in construction (carpenter, bricklayer, electrician, etc., who work together to build a single house).

In terms of structure, this type of team functions in the same way as a team where all staff perform the same role.

However, working as part of a multidisciplinary team is sometimes more difficult, because some specialists tend to interfere in their colleagues' fields. Sometimes the colleague's knowledge and expertise is even called into question. This can easily develop into a battle, either hidden or overt, sometimes at the cost of the results and the atmosphere at work. When team members respect each other's fields and take advantage of each other's expertise, then there's not a problem.

Multidisciplinary approach and authority

In some cases, one of the team members has more of a say than the others by virtue of the job he does. For example, in a health care team a psychiatrist legally bears final responsibility for patients' treatment. In principle this can mean that he has veto rights in decision-making, or is able to make an independent decision on the patient's treatment method. It works better when the other team members are involved and can join in the discussion about determining the method, thus creating support. Perhaps the psychiatrist also needs to make some concessions in the treatment proposal, meaning that the other team members are more motivated to carry it out.

OVERLOAD, A NEGATIVE EFFECT OF SELF-MANAGEMENT?

We often hear that a disadvantage of self-management is that team members get overloaded. Team members themselves say that they sometimes have to take too much onto their plates since beginning self-management. It is indeed something that happens sometimes, but we would prefer not to call it a disadvantage of self-management.

In a self-managing team, the team members feel jointly responsible for the activities they need to carry out. Sometimes, however, absenteeism due to illness increases (temporarily) or there is (also temporarily) a bit more work to do, and then we see that the team members have no problem with stepping up the pace – precisely because they feel a sense of responsibility. But sometimes the phase in which extra effort is required goes on for too long, meaning that the pressure of work is too high and work-life balance is disturbed.

This then requires good consultation on the amount of activities assigned. It's important here to respect the capacity of the individual employee. This doesn't always happen; some team members are annoyed that their colleagues are not always able to go the extra mile, and they place pressure on these members of the team. This results in even more stress, in addition to overload caused by the extra work.

The solution to preventing overloading therefore lies in accepting each other's capacities for work. If this then means that the team does not possess sufficient capacity to perform the work, the coach and/or manager will need to assist the team to find other options. It's also important that the coach and the manager respect the employee's limits, because absenteeism due to overloading is waiting down the track. If that happens, nobody will benefit.

MEETING OF TEAM REPRESENTATIVES

In practice, topics which are discussed in a number of teams frequently require co-ordination, for example things like the PR policy, safety, training, and curriculum development. These need to be co-ordinated in order to enable clear communication with clients, referrers or municipalities.

Sometimes a team member wants to undertake further personal development, has gained a lot of knowledge of a particular topic, and is keen to assist other teams in that field; for example, he might want to develop a training session in collaboration with colleagues from other teams.

These are great initiatives, but they can become a problem periodic consultations are held with one or more representatives from each team. Decisions are often made during these consultations, which is already a bit of a problem in itself considering how self-management is meant to work. The representatives end up making decisions for the other teams, thus creating a new hierarchical layer. In self-management the intention is actually that decision-making power rests within the teams, and that each team can make its own decisions within the organizational frameworks.

Teams that work closely with each other can certainly find it useful to consult each other, but this should only be done when necessary – i.e. not periodically, because then it becomes an 'institution'. And the employees who attend that meeting should not be given a mandate because they then run the risk of 'deciding for others'.

PITFALL OF REINTEGRATION FOLLOWING ILLNESS

Illness may mean that a team member is absent from work for a longer period of time. Sometimes the others then notice that team collaboration is much more enjoyable, and start to make comments about it: 'It's only now that you really see the influence Jenny has on the meeting', or 'Sorting out the roster ourselves is actually much nicer now', and 'It's so peaceful now that Richard's not here'. At a certain point the whole team ends up discussing the inplications of these observations, and the team coach is often involved in these discussions too. Before they know it, the team have come up with all kinds of conditions with which the absent colleague will have to comply when he comes back. In addition, the coach is often told that it would be better if the colleague started his reintegration on another team.

In this case, the team members are not taking responsibility for their earlier behaviour. They may have seen the effect that the team member had on the team's functioning before he got sick, but no-one made the effort to discuss the behaviour with him. Or perhaps the behaviour only became more obvious once the team member was away on sick leave. In both cases the team members should organise for the sick colleague to be reintegrated as part of their own team, and to discuss the difficult behaviour with him at a later point.

The team member concerned then has the opportunity to change his behaviour and together the team members can ensure that their teamwork improves.

Factors in successful self-management

If obviously present, these criteria more or less guarantee that a self-managing team will function optimally.

- The team works within clear frameworks which were agreed on with the management.
- The team has the authority to make their own decisions, within the agreed frameworks.
- A self-managing team is an evenly balanced team, with people who are prepared to 'give in'.
- There is agreement on the division of labour.
- The team regularly holds effective discussions, where a solution-oriented approach is used and decisions are made by consensus.
- In addition to their individual professional responsibilities, the team members feel jointly responsible for the organizational tasks and the team results.
- The team members get along well with each other and are happy with the team.
- The team achieves good results.
- Within the team, the individual members can be approached if the quality of their work is not up to scratch, and they noticeably do their best to improve.
- The team can rely on good support from the coach.

7

The Solution Driven Method of Interaction (SDMI®) and self-management

If you want to treat people equally, you have to approach them differently.
– Astrid Vermeer and Ben Wenting –

Another way of supporting self-management within an organization is by paying attention to how its members communicate. The ideal is a communication style in which equality, encouraging responsibility and problem-solving are more important than placing blame, acknowledging mistakes, and decisions based on power. A style that concrete enough to allow all members of the organization can apply it easily, but that nonetheless offers so many possibilities that it can also be used to solve complex problems.

The Solution Driven Method of Interaction® (SDMI®) is a methodology with these features. Simply being familiar with a methodology is obviously no guarantee of success; a methodology only has value when it is applied in a way that suits the nature of the user. Many people are introduced to all sorts of discussion and communication methodologies but don't use them, or not in the right way, and then say that the methodology is no good. 'People know what they should do, but they don't do it.'

In this chapter we outline the basics of the SDMI® and provide examples of how to apply it.

DISTINGUISHING BETWEEN PROBLEM-ORIENTED AND SOLUTION-ORIENTED WORKING

SDMI® is a solution-oriented methodology: it takes the current situation, the present, as a starting point, and uses that to consider solutions in the future.

There are also problem-oriented methodologies. These first investigate the problem, look for its causes, and then look for solutions on the basis of this information. In problem-oriented methodology you also look at who is to 'blame', what you no longer want, or what you want to avoid. Solution-oriented working means that you look chiefly at what you *do* want: what can you do to improve a situation, and who or what is needed in order to achieve that?

This makes the SDMI® an optimistic and non-judgmental (you don't try to place 'blame') method that fits well with the vision behind self-organization. In a self-managing organization, the team members and managers are expected to be able to respond effectively to developments in the team and 'on the market', and a decisive, future-oriented attitude is in keeping with this. Decisiveness is also associated with thoroughness, efficiency, speed, extroversion and so on. However, in this case we're referring to decisiveness in the sense of 'decision-making ability'. Sometimes it's not fast and decisive at all, but takes time to properly formulate what needs to be done differently in the future. Nonetheless, it works towards 'reaching a decision' and not 'coming up with a good description of the problem'. The first of these stimulates thinking up solutions, the second stimulates diagnosing the problem and thereby identifying causes that need to be cleared up or avoided in the future.

The SDMI® assumes that your historical data and descriptions of problems are usually not necessary in order to come up with a sensible way of thinking of solutions in the future. In addition, it is human nature to try to resolve uncomfortable situations as quickly as possible so that everyone feels comfortable again. Finding solutions to problems – quickly – and adapting to inevitable changes is probably one of the things that has brought the human race to where we are now. Finding solutions is faster and more efficient if you first determine your goal, then look at how you can get there, and then decide on the best course of action.

Problem-oriented methodologies focus on analysing the past; the SDMI® analyses the current and future situations and a plan of action is developed based on these. Analysing the past is sometimes useful if a path towards finding a solution can't be found immediately.

THE PRINCIPLES OF SDMI®

The SDMI® is based on a view of human nature. This view is based on a number of assumptions, which we explain below.

Conscious choices and responsibility

The SDMI® assumes that people are able to make *conscious choices* and are therefore able to take *responsibility* for their actions.

Making choices is obviously not always done consciously; people often make choices based on feelings. Sometimes you don't know exactly why you want something, you just 'feel' that it's a good idea. And yet, if you take the time to pause and reflect on that feeling, you can often become more aware of the reasons why you want or do something. The more you make choices consciously, the less things 'happen' to you and the less you end up being surprised by unexpected consequences. We seem to like that ...

Organization members (those who execute the primary process, and managers) taking responsibility is one of the pillars of a self-managing organization.

The reverse also works. If you want people to take responsibility, they need to have the opportunity – and thus the power – to make choices. It's only when they have the power that they can be held accountable for their choices. This means that self-management (the teams bearing responsibility for the results) isn't possible if they don't have a great deal of decision-making power. In other words: if a team doesn't have the opportunity to make the decisions that are necessary in order for them to do their jobs well, there is no question of self-management.

We assume that people *can* take responsibility, but that doesn't mean that they always *want* to take it. Obviously being held responsible for something is not always a good thing, because it means that you can also be held accountable for the consequences, and that's definitely not always an appealing prospect. Responsibility goes hand in hand with *accountability*.

Respect

Respect is another premise on which the SDMI® is based. And we're not talking about others addressing you as 'Mr' or 'Ms', or the commonly-heard phase 'With all due respect', ... followed by a condemnation of the previous speaker.

By 'respect', we mean the wholehearted acceptance of differences between people. As everyone knows, everyone's different. Some people are doers, others thinkers, initiative-takers or followers, beautiful or ugly, Christian or Hindu. We assume that everyone has something meaningful to contribute to a discussion, based on their own background, character or abilities. It's only once you accept this that you are able to be receptive to your colleagues and to collaborate on an equal basis, whether those colleagues are fellow team members, managers, or supporting staff. That doesn't mean that people are all the same. Of course there is a difference between people and their roles. Position, character and education or training result in differences, meaning that one person is more suited than another to certain tasks and activities. But that doesn't mean that someone therefore 'deserves' a lower or higher position as a person. This is an important basis for working in a self-organization. When you have respect for all members of the organization, people are aware that you're not passing judgement on them and everyone feels free to say what they think.

Active energy

The SDMI® assumes that when we end up in a situation that we experience as unpleasant, we take action. We want to feel comfortable again as soon as possible. That means that we automatically try to think of ways to solve the problem, rather than going into how it came about. We move towards the future. This is why the SDMI® is a solution-oriented method, not a problem-oriented one.

The majority of people focus on constructive ways to get rid of the problem, and a few will choose a way that may be comfortable for the team member but may not always be constructive in their colleagues' eyes. One example might be colleagues who blame their mistakes on external factors. These people actually look after themselves well, and in their own way they generate a certain type of 'active energy' to solve their problem; they actively turn away from the problem.

It's more difficult when one colleague has a problem and wants to find a solution, and the other colleague doesn't have that problem. It may even be in his interest to leave the problem with his colleague. In that case he won't want to put a lot of energy into helping to solve his colleague's problem. The colleague with the problem could then first consider whether or not he actually needs the other person.

WORKING WITH THE SDMI®: 5 POINTS TO NOTE

The principles mentioned earlier are given a concrete, workable form in these five points. The points play a more or less prominent role in every situation, they are interrelated, and they enable insight into the situation, how to deal with it and to make (as far as is possible) well-considered decisions, if necessary.

For team members (and sometimes managers), making decisions and taking responsibility is something that they sometimes have to master (it's different for everyone). The hierarchical work situation offered few opportunities for this.

Using the points to prepare for discussions or situations that call for change highlights all of the aspects that play a role. In a discussion, too, the points can help to enable insight into situations, so goal-oriented adjustments can be made and the team can stay 'on track'.

The five points are:

1 *Goal*: what do you want to achieve?
2 *Position*: what do you have responsibility for? What can you decide for yourself? What can't you? What are your skills?
3 *Working method*: how are you going to achieve your goal?
4 *Communication method*: communicating with each other in a respectful, clear and direct way.

5 *Time*: how much time do you have to achieve your goal – is there a deadline? How much time do you need?

We will examine these in more detail one by one.

Goal

If you employ SDMI®, one of the first questions you ask at the moment that a problem or issue arises is: 'What do I want to achieve?'

This point is therefore directly related to the method's solution-oriented character. If there's no goal, there's no direction. In other words, without a goal you just do whatever. That usually doesn't achieve much. Making the goal clear and concrete allows you to determine whether the proposed actions are in line with the goal.

We often see that goals are formulated negatively: 'We want to ensure that no more customers switch over to the competition', or 'employees should spend less time on administration'. This focuses your thinking on something that you don't want, making it more likely that you'll choose 'negative' solutions.

We will go on to discuss the reasons why customers switch to the competition, as well as how that could be prevented. The competitor might have lower prices, so you then lower your price too. For example, when the issue is 'employees should spend less time on administration', the positive goal formulation becomes: 'Employees need to spend more time on clients'.

When you formulate your goal positively, you say what you *do* want to achieve and you focus your thinking on positive solutions. The goal then becomes 'to engage our current customers', and then you will probably come up with other solutions. Perhaps you then come up with a marketing strategy designed to raise awareness of the organization's specialty, or the employees are instructed to manage customers differently.

A 'means' is often raised to a 'goal'. I want to achieve the procurement of a new coffee machine. However, procuring a new machine is a means of obtaining good coffee. Good coffee is therefore also the goal that you want to achieve, and perhaps there are other means of achieving that than via the procurement of another machine.

Position

In addition to determining the goal, it's important to know who is authorised to achieve the objective, and capable of achieving it. In the 'customer engagement' example, the field worker and the marketing specialist may be the most capable of coming up with solutions.

Another example: for health care professionals who need to spend more time on clients (and less on administration), it's probably a good idea to consult the health care professionals to find out why they spend so much time on administration. Administrative staff can then be asked how they might be able to contribute to reducing administrative pressure on the health care workers.

Working method

Once it's clear what needs to be accomplished and who is involved, the ways of realising that goal can be discussed.

To return to the previous example for a moment: 'Employees need to spend more time on clients'. What are some ways of achieving that goal? It may indeed involve 'reducing administrative pressure', but taking on more caregivers might also be an option. Perhaps reporting could be made more efficient, so that the caregivers have fewer forms they have to fill out?

Communication method

When dealing with other people, it's important to communicate clearly, directly and respectfully – and for the other person to communicate with you in the same manner. The better you know what you want and why, the easier it is to be clear. The clearer you are, the easier it is for your conversation partner to respond, and for the two of you to arrive at mutually satisfactory agreements. If the person you're talking to isn't clear about what he expects of you, it's difficult for you to make a choice – so it's important that you ask the other person to be clear.

A clear and direct manner of communication contributes to an equal, respectful and therefore enjoyable working relationship. It's about the little things: a colleague comes to you and asks if he can have the day off the day after tomorrow. You both know that there's an important team meeting scheduled on that day – and it was very difficult to organize. You could say, 'Well, if a day off is more important to you than the meeting, it's up to you, it's your responsibility'. Your colleague then has to read between the lines to see that you don't agree, and you might be hoping that he feels so guilty about it that he'll just come to the meeting. It's clearer and more direct, and puts you on a more equal footing, to say, 'I'm really not keen on that idea. It was really hard to schedule a date for the meeting. I value your opinion, and then we'd miss out on it. Would you be able to take a different day off instead?'

Because you clearly indicate how you feel about it and give the reason why you want him to come to the meeting, your colleague is able to make a decision based on what's actually going on, and not based on a negative feeling because he feels manipulated.

Time

When working with the SDMI®, 'time' is an important factor to consider. 'Time' is a given within the organization and is not always easy to influence. There's often a deadline, and problems often have to be solved within a certain time frame or else other members of the organization will suffer negative consequences.

Time constraints mean that problems can't always be resolved in the most desirable way. You might prefer to have the vacancy filled by someone with a Higher Professional Education diploma who has at least ten years' experience, wants to work 36 hours, and can start next week. But if none of the candidates fits this profile and there's no time to keep on looking, then something in the goal or the working method needs to change in order to allow you to move forward. Perhaps the Higher Professional Education with less experience is good enough, or someone with an intermediate vocational education and lots of experience would also be satisfactory.

The 'time' factor therefore has a great deal of influence on the way the other factors are interpreted.

NO SET ORDER

The five points don't need to be followed in a set order. It's certainly advisable to first consider the goal that needs to be achieved, but later in the discussion or when making an action plan you can look at which point needs to be considered at that stage. In meetings it's not uncommon for, say, an agreement to be made to purchase from company X in the future, because it's cheaper and offers the same quality (goal), but no agreement is made about who will cancel the current supplier (position), and when that will happen (time).

A NEW 'NOW' EVERY TIME

Sometimes you can see that in retrospect, an action or agreement didn't have the desired effect, or no longer suits the situation that has developed. You might then be inclined to continue along the agreed path, because suddenly changing your opinion might seem stupid, unstable or fickle. It's also not always easy to admit that you evaluated a situation incorrectly, and it feels like you have to go 'grovelling' back to your colleagues, so you just keep on down the same track and hope for the best.

The earlier decision, however, was made to the best of your ability with the knowledge you had available at that time. If you could have foreseen that the decision wouldn't have the desired effect, you would obviously have made a different choice. There's no blame on you.

When applying the SDMI®, you assume that every new moment is a new 'now' and that new choices can be made based on the new insights gained. You're never stuck in the past and you're always able to respond effectively to current developments.

THE SDMI®'S APPLICABILITY IN PRACTICE

The methodology only truly comes into focus when we see how it works in practice. There are a number of examples on YouTube; instructions for finding them are included at the back of this book.

We will also give some examples here to show how to work with the SDMI® focus points.

Team member addresses another team member about her working method

A team agreed that team member Sarah would be responsible for the team task of 'procuring office supplies' for the location concerned. However, Sarah has a small contract so is not at work that often and often has external appointments when working. This means that office supplies aren't topped up regularly, causing Walter problems with his own work. Walter decides to talk to Sarah about it. First he thinks about what he's going to say. He uses the five focus points for this:

Goal

What does he actually want to achieve? He wants there to always be sufficient stocks of all office supplies.
And not, as might seem obvious: I want Sarah to order the supplies on time. That says something about Sarah (position) and when the supplies should be ordered (time).
His position therefore expresses his intention.

Position

Sarah is responsible for the task, so he needs to speak to her to see whether she can take care of it.

Working method

He's not going to think about how his goal will be achieved, because Sarah is the one performing the task, so it's up to her to determine how she will make sure that the supplies are kept stocked.

Communication method

He communicates this to her clearly.

>>

>>

Time

Walter doesn't want to find that things have run out again, so that's what he wants regarding the 'time' focus point. It is then up to Sarah to organize the time aspect in a way that ensures that the supplies are always kept stocked.

The discussion might go like this:
Walter: 'Sarah, from now on could you make sure that all the office supplies are kept stocked please? I'm often left staring at an empty shelf, and it's really annoying. You're in charge of that task, so would you be able to take care of it?'
Sarah: 'Yes, that's obviously not how it's meant to work. You've brought it up before, or I've heard you complaining about it, but because I'm not in the office that much I can't keep an eye on the stock levels.'
Walter: 'What can you do to solve that?' (working method)
Sarah: 'I don't know, I can't really come in more often. Sometimes I'm nowhere near the office ...'
Walter: 'Do you think it's practical for you to be in charge of that task?' (position)
Sarah: 'Not really, no. It would be better if someone who's in the office more often took care of it.'
Walter: 'What would you propose?'
Sarah: 'At the next meeting, I'll raise the point that it's difficult for me to perform this task, and propose that someone else takes care of it in future.'
Walter: 'Thanks for working with me on this.'

A team asks a trainer a question

A team asks the trainer to provide a course on communication techniques, because their teamwork has had a few hiccups lately.

>>

>>

The trainer could take this request and develop an interesting three-day programme. When he – using the five focus points – looks into the team's question in more detail, the following conversation might result:

Trainer: 'What do you want to achieve with a course in communication techniques?' (goal)

Team member: 'That things in our team run more smoothly.'

Trainer: 'What's in need of improvement in your team?' (goal)

Team member: 'We need to stop constantly clipping each other's wings; we don't let each other shine.'

Trainer: 'What do you need to learn then?' (goal)

Team member: 'Well ... we need to learn to respect each other as we are, and to appreciate each other more for the qualities that each of us possesses.'

Trainer: (thinks: 'I still don't know exactly why they want a communication course', and continues asking questions) 'What would need to happen in the course then, that would mean that you do better? From what you're saying, you know exactly what needs to change.' (goal)

Team member: 'Yes, that's true, but we can't talk to each other about it, it always ends up in an argument.'

Trainer: 'And what would a course be able to change about that?' (goal)

Team member: 'That we'd know what's wrong.'

Trainer: 'But don't you know that already?' (goal)

Team member: 'Yes, we do, but we don't talk about it.'

Trainer: 'Then I would suggest that you talk to each other about it. That might be more relevant to the problem than if you take a training course but don't actually sit and talk to each other.' (working method)

Team member: 'No, maybe not, but could you help us with a discussion about it?'

Trainer: 'I think that's more of a question for the team coach.' (position) >>

>> Team member: 'Then I'll discuss it with the team, and we'll ask the team coach.'

In this example it's obvious that the team members often come up with a way of solving a problem, without being clear on the aim. As long as the goal remains unclear, the trainer asks questions to help achieve clarity. The other points are then less important. Once the goal is clear, the other focus points can help to further answer the question.

Manager discusses a team's progress. There are many client complaints about the quality of care
The Care manager has noticed that in the past six months there has been a higher than average number of complaints about this team, and he wants the team to be able to discuss it.
He, too, thinks beforehand about what exactly he wants to achieve with the discussion, what powers he has, the powers that the team has, and whether he already has ideas about the working method and the time.

A brief sketch of the conversation:
Manager: 'As you know, I receive quite a lot of complaints about your team, and that's not good. I'd like to see fewer complaints coming in. What do you think about that?' (goal)
Team: 'Yes, we're obviously not happy about it either and we're doing everything we can to reduce the number of complaints. The problem is that a few of us are sick, and if we want to care for all the clients, we're only able to do that by doing just the things that are most needed, and then quickly going off to the next patient.'
Manager: 'Yes, the complaints are about the rush, but there are also more mistakes being reported than usual, meaning >>

>> that we're not providing the quality that people have come to expect from us. Do you have some ideas about how you can ensure that you can deliver the required quality and avoid mistakes?' (goal and working method)

Team: 'No, actually, because the people who are sick haven't come back yet, and we're not permitted to hire temp workers, and the other departments are all busy too – and obviously we can't just kick the patients out. We really feel like our hands are tied on this one.'

Manager: 'I can imagine. But I'd still really like to see some improvement. What would help you to see a ray of hope again?' (working method)

Team: 'Perhaps someone else has some ideas that we haven't thought of yet, or there's someone who can make the decision to make changes to our agreements. It would be a great help to us if we could use more on-call workers for the evening shifts. Pauline has back problems and can't do any care work, but perhaps she could offer administrative support. That would save us a lot of time that we can then spend with patients.'

Manager: 'As far as I'm concerned you can use on-call staff (position), and I think asking Pauline to help you is a good idea. I'd also like to suggest that you keep talking about this with your coach, and that she takes a look at what other options there might be. If you need the HR staff, then you can obviously involve them too. When can I expect a proposal on how you plan to improve the quality of your work?' (working method and time)

Team: 'We need to deal with this quickly. How about next week?'

Manager: 'Great. If you need anything else from me then just let me know.' (position)

The manager leaves the responsibility for the solution to the team, but indicates the frameworks within which the team is expected to operate.

The coach discusses the meeting structure with the team
The team ask the coach to come and discuss the meetings with them. The team members feel that the discussions are too drawn out.

Here's a brief sketch of this discussion:
Coach: 'What can I do for you to help you improve your meetings?' (position)
Team: 'Our discussions go on for so long, and we almost never manage to make decisions. We've got no idea what we're doing wrong.'
Coach: 'Perhaps it would help if I take a look at exactly how your meetings go? Perhaps then I can give some advice, so that you can improve your meetings?' (coach gives advice regarding his own role; does the method correspond with the goal?)
Team: 'Good idea, we have an important topic on the agenda.'
Coach: 'Then I suggest that while you're working on that point, I say what I think could be done differently, so you can try it right away.'
Team: 'Let's get started!'

8
Solution-oriented meetings

I met a man who had a dollar.
We exchanged dollars. We each still had a dollar.
Then I met a man who had an idea.
We exchanged ideas.
Now we each have two ideas.
– The Optimism Revolution –

The team meeting is an important moment for a self-managing team. It's when the team members come together to discuss the work and its execution, so it needs to be constructive and enjoyable.

Common complaints about meetings include: it's too long-winded, too chaotic, it's always the same people talking, nobody listens to me, 'they' just decide to do what they want to do ... Meetings can be a bit too much about 'who's right', and 'who calls the shots'. They're a power play.

In this chapter we discuss what the meeting model based on the SDMI® can contribute to the smooth running of meetings.

The SDMI® meeting model is given in full at the end of this chapter, and we include an illustration of how it is used in practice.

We will begin by discussing a number of aspects of meetings, and how the SDMI® meeting model approaches these.

'ANY OTHER BUSINESS?'

The 'Any other business' segment is a regular part of the meeting, usually the last item on the agenda. The attendees can ask questions about current issues: *short question, short answer* ... However, during the meeting there is rarely a simple answer available. Colleagues have opinions on the matter too and seemed to be a simple question at first ends up turning into a serious discussion. These issues are often urgent, so an answer needs to be found during the meeting. As a result, to everyone's great annoyance, the meeting runs over time. Team members who have to go to their next appointment end up leaving, so they can't participate in any agreements that might be made.

This problem is fairly easy to solve, by looking at 'any other business' at the start of the meeting. People can ask their questions and if a short answer is sufficient, then it's sorted. If a discussion develops, the point can be added to the provisional agenda.

SCHEDULING TIME FOR EACH ITEM ON THE AGENDA

Most agendas don't schedule time for each item; people simply talk for as long as they need to. Sometimes that can be a long time, and as a result they don't get through the whole agenda. This is easily solved by scheduling time for each topic. The person who introduces the topic also gives the expected duration.

If the total time required for the topics is longer than the allocated meeting time, a check will be made to see which points can be saved for the following meeting, which points will require less time, or whether people think it's a good idea for the meeting to last a bit longer so that all the tabled issues can be dealt with.

The person who tabled an issue is the one to decide whether or not to postpone it or to shorten the amount of time scheduled to discuss the item. If this person wants to extend the meeting time, all team members must agree to this in order for it to go ahead.

In this model, therefore, the chair is not the one who determines how the meeting time will be used.

PROGRESS AND TOPIC DECISIONS

One of the characteristics of the SDMI® meeting model is that distinguishes between progress decisions and topic decisions.

Topic decisions relate to the items on the agenda that are discussed at the meeting, and are therefore about the substance of the work. These decisions are made at the end of dealing with an item on the agenda.

Progress decisions, however, can be made at any time during the meeting. These are the decisions that the team makes together in order to regulate the meeting's progress. Progress decisions are not inventoried like topic decisions are, but if the chair or a team member makes a progress proposal then it is immediately put to the vote. If, for example, the time allocated to a topic has finished but the topic has not yet been concluded, a team member can say, 'I propose that we spend another ten minutes on this point, then we can conclude it.' The chair then asks, 'Who is in agreement?' If there is consensus (nobody objects), then a further ten minutes will be spent on the item. If not, then the original time allocation will be enforced and the meeting will move to the next item on the agenda.

In most meetings, the chair makes progress decisions. However, this means that he or she has a big say in how the meeting progresses, leaving the other attendees with less influence. This can lead to the attendees becoming passive.

To allow all attendees to have the same degree of influence on the meeting's progress, it's advisable to have progress decisions decided collectively (by consensus).

> A progress proposal concerns an amendment to the previously agreed time schedule, and goes to the vote immediately. If there is no consensus for the proposal, then the meeting continues according to the agenda determined previously.

HANDLING ITEMS ON THE AGENDA

In the previous chapter we discussed the importance of goal-setting: where do you want to go, what do you want to achieve, what has to be solved? The same applies to handling items on the agenda. The point added to the agenda is usually too broadly formulated. For example: the budget, collaborating with the administrative department, holiday planning, the roster, training, new products.

This broad formulation means that each team member develops his or her own picture of the topic, and the discussion is conducted based on this. These pictures are not always related to the issue that the person who introduced the topic actually wants to address. As a result the discussion can go in any direction and at the end of it all, the person who submitted the item is sometimes left empty-handed: his problem hasn't been solved. Perhaps other problems have been, but that wasn't his goal.

It's also difficult for the chair, because when should she intervene? When is a comment still related to the subject at hand, and when not?

Replacing agenda topics with questions or suggestions indicates a clear direction for the subsequent discussion.

'The budget' could for example become: 'When can the budget be finalised?'

'Good co-operation with the administration' becomes 'I propose that the administration department is staffed on Friday afternoons until 4pm.'

'Holiday planning' becomes 'Can I take my holidays in the first week of May?' 'Training' becomes 'How are we going to schedule our training sessions in the coming year?', and 'the roster' becomes 'How are we going to balance our roster, now that three of the ten team members have been felled by the flu?'

It may be that Mary also has a question that falls under the agenda item 'How are we going to schedule our training sessions in the coming year?' Her question is: 'When can I schedule my internship for the course I'm currently studying?' This question would normally just be discussed immediately, but in the SDMI® meeting model the questions (which don't actually have anything to do with each other) will be dealt with separately. It's only then that every point receives the attention it deserves, and the issues don't get confused.

This allows the attendees to all focus on the same question, and the chair can easily tell whether someone is straying from it.

In addition to knowing how to formulate the question or proposal, attendees need to know how much of a say they have on a topic. The organizational frameworks generally indicate whether the team has decision-making powers or whether these rest with someone else. If the team holds these powers, they can make the decision together. If the powers rest with, for example, the manager, then the team can put forward their opinion, but the manager will be the one to make the decision. If a team discusses a subject believing that they hold decision-making powers, it's exceptionally frustrating to have these removed later on.

By extension, the purpose of discussing an agenda item can be stated too. Sometimes an employee has questions about his work, and wants to know what he can improve. For example, he might ask: 'How can I deal with aggressive clients?' The aim of handling this during the meeting is to enable him to obtain advice from his colleagues.

Finally, an item can be added to the agenda simply for 'information'. Peter went to a symposium and wants to tell his colleagues about it. Obviously his colleagues can ask questions, but there's no need for them to come up with suggestions or to make decisions.

The formulation of the question or proposal, the reason (why is the item on the agenda), and where the authority lies are submitted by the person who raises the topic, and the agreement of other team members is not required.

When dealing with a question, there are a number of possible answers. The chair asks what these are, the arguments, and the consequences of the suggestions. During the discussion, the proposals are inventoried before being put to the vote. The team members then have time to compare the proposals and to discuss them with each other in detail. This gives the space required to enable an in-depth discussion. When considering a proposal, the arguments for or against are given. The proposal is only put to the vote once all the pros and cons have been covered.

In the SDMI® meeting model, the discussion doesn't automatically progress to decision-making. The attendees make a joint decision as to whether they're ready to decide; have all the suggestions been noted and have we been able to consider them all carefully? This gives peace of mind during the discussion. This also allows the 'slower' (but often very serious) thinkers to be taken into account.

NOT SUMMARIES, BUT QUESTIONS

Almost all courses on meetings and chairing teach that the chair sums up the discussion, and finishes with a concluding summary. However, summarising discussions has a number of drawbacks:

- it takes up a lot of time, because everything you summarise has already been said;
- it brings things to a halt, because nothing new happens during a summary;
- it makes the participants passive, because the participants don't have to structure it themselves;
- Some suggestions 'disappear', because it's impossible to place conflicting opinions together in a single summary. This gives the chair the ability to steer (intentionally or unintentionally) the discussion considerably;
- Summaries are never an accurate reflection of *everything* that was said in a discussion (see the previous point) and therefore provoke opposition in the participants. After a summary is given, the discussion often turns to 'disputing' that summary, which can push the substance of the topic into the background.

For these reasons, the SDMI® meeting model teaches the chair (and the participants) to ask solution-oriented questions. This stimulates participants' involvement, and the chair doesn't risk steering the discussion.

The questions that the chair can ask are included in the SDMI® meeting model at the end of this chapter. She can also use these questions to promote deeper examination of the issues during the discussion.

Solution proposals are inventoried and preferably written down on a flip chart. Everyone can see the suggestions made, so the chair no longer needs to summarise the discussion.

PROPOSAL-BASED DECISION-MAKING

When there are no new proposals and the arguments have all been discussed, all proposals will be put to the vote one by one. Each team member can vote for multiple proposals, so they are more likely to be flexible in terms of giving in on certain points. This makes it easier to reach a consensus.

There's no need to ask who's against a proposal, because only the proposals for which everyone votes will be adopted. The others are automatically discarded. The point is that proposals are adopted which are supported by the entire team.

Sometimes one member really doesn't support a proposal that the rest of the team endorses. If a little time is spent on addressing that person's main objection, then the team might come up with something which will remove that objection. It may be a good idea to make an exception to the proposal just for that team member. This, too, is consensus: taking a colleague's specific situation into account. For example, if the team would like to agree that shifts will start at 7am, but it's impossible for a single mother in the team to find child care for that time, then you might decide that her shifts won't start until 8am. Obviously everyone needs to support the exceptions.

NONE OF THE PROPOSALS ARE ADOPTED

Above we have assumed that one or more of the proposals will be adopted. At times none of the proposals will be endorsed by everyone. What happens then? It's very simple: people can't agree on a new agreement, so everything stays as it is. This could mean that the earlier agreement stays the same, even though not everyone is happy with it. If no agreement has yet been made on that particular topic then the situation will remain the same. The only difference is that in such cases the team members won't go on to act on the basis of an earlier agreement, but according to their own discretion.

A teaching team, for example, might consider the agenda item: 'How can the dyslexic students be assisted when doing tests?'

Previously there was no agreement about this. If no proposal is adopted during the meeting, then each teacher will continue to assist students in their own way.

Sometimes it's essential that everyone agrees, for example when an agreement needs to be made on taking action in line with the organization's vision, or working with quality criteria.

DECISION-MAKING AND ABSENCE

Employees in self-managing teams are generally highly motivated and absenteeism is often low. But even on these teams, team members are sometimes absent due to illness or holidays. As decisions are made by consensus, it's important that everyone has a say. The team members could make an agreement on the way in which absentees can still take part in decision-making. If there's no agreement in place, you run the risk of the absentee disagreeing with a decision and bringing up the discussion again at a later time.

How can you involve absentees in decision-making? They can give their opinions in advance, and if the proposals match the opinions that they have put forward, the decision can be made during the meeting. When very different proposals are put to the vote at the meeting, the decision will be made at the following meeting. The absentee can then join in the vote.

Another option is to allow absentees to vote after the meeting based on the minutes, which include the proposals and the arguments for these.

Then, too, it can be agreed that decisions will be made only when everyone is present. When someone is absent, a decision will not be made until the following meeting (this is not always possible in larger teams, because there's always someone absent).

Absentees can also ask another team member to vote on their behalf. They then choose someone who has more or less the same opinions.

There are undoubtedly more options. Whichever one is chosen, the premise remains that everyone should have the opportunity to participate in decision-making.

DIFFICULT MEETING SITUATIONS

During meetings there are always situations in which one participant behaves in a way which is not easy for the others to deal with: constantly repeating their own viewpoint, going on about their own pet topic, talking over other attendees, etc.

The other attendees get annoyed, and the level of irritation gets so high that the troublemaker can't miss the fact that he's being annoying. This is usually not pleasant for anyone involved.

The SDMI® meeting model makes it easy to defuse these difficult situations. We discuss some of the methods below.

Repetition

For whatever reason, the team member seems to think that he needs to keep repeating his opinion. It takes up a lot of time, and it's boring. The 'repeater' is often put in his place in an agitated tone: 'Peter, we heard you the first five times ...'

However, when the proposals are written down on a flip chart and are visible to everyone, the tendency to repeat is dramatically reduced. The repeater, too, can see that his proposal has been noted. If he keeps going, then questions like 'Is this a different proposal from what's been made already?', or 'Do you have any *other* proposals or arguments?' are very effective in stopping the repeater.

Derails

Some team members are very good at free-associating, and they bring up these associations in the discussion. When talking about planning the summer holidays, they may suddenly ask a question about taking on new work during the summer when there are only minimal staff present. Others may find it logical to include this in the discussion and discuss it in more depth. Before long the discussion is no longer about planning the summer holidays, but about whether or not to take on new work when there are few staff present, for example due to illness ... obviously a derail.

The discussion can be brought back to the agenda item by asking the derailer: 'Can you explain to me how this is related to the topic at hand?' The derailer will have to acknowledge that there's no connection, and you can then return to the original discussion.

Pet topics

Some people – and therefore some team members – manage to bring up their favourite topic (for example, 'equal opportunities for everyone') on every item on the agenda. So the training policy, hiring a new colleague, or the distribution of organizational tasks within the team becomes an opportunity to hold forth on how 'it's so important that everyone has the chance to get an education/is able to apply/should be able to do the task'.

Content-based questions can be asked here too, so that the team member keeps to the subject but still feels that he is being treated with respect. For example, you could ignore his opinion on equal rights and simply ask him, 'Do you have a proposal regarding the distribution of our training budget?' This prevents a discussion on the relevance of equal rights, and gently brings the derailer back to the item on the agenda.

Chaos

Chaos occurs when a number of team members talk over each other. In this type of situation, many chairs call out, 'Can everyone stay focused please', but this is a very general statement and nobody feels like they're being personally addressed.

It's more effective to address the team member who's causing the most disturbance by name, and only to ask for a proposal once you have his attention.

The chair therefore doesn't resolve the situations above by calling the disruptive behaviour to order (which is what usually happens). The chair's irritation and discussing the disruptive behaviour mostly results in an argument. Chairs can verbalise their irritation as follows:

- 'I'm finding it irritating that you keep repeating your viewpoint. This isn't going to move us forward.'
- 'See what happens when you all talk over each other?'

- ‘You should talk about your own principles a bit less – can’t you see that your colleagues are getting irritated?’

These types of comments generally make team members feel that they’re being personally criticised, which doesn’t stimulate them to act differently during the meeting.

In our opinion it’s better not to make a big fuss about the behaviour, but instead to ask a substantive question, which allows the disruptor to make a positive contribution to the meeting.

EXPLANATION OF THE SDMI® MEETING MODEL

The complete meeting structure based on the SDMI® can be summarised in a model (see below). A brief explanation may help you to fully understand the model.

SDMI meeting model®

Fixed agenda items

1a Discussion of the minutes on the last meeting (textual)
1b Announcements
1c Any other business

Determining the definitive agenda

2a What are the additions to the agenda, and how much time is required to deal with them?

When there are too many agenda items for the available meeting time

2b Who has suggestions for:
- postponing his agenda item
- reducing the time required to deal with his agenda item
- extending the meeting time

Dealing with the agenda items (follow points 3 to 10 for each item on the agenda)

>>

>> *Introduction of the agenda item*

3 Which question or suggestion do you want to deal with?
4 Why are you making this proposal or asking this question?
5 Would you like to share or receive information, give advice, or make a decision? (What authority do the meeting and/or attendees have?)

Discussion

6 Who has a proposal?
What arguments do you have in its favour?
What do the others think of the proposal and the arguments?
What are the advantages and disadvantages of the proposal?
What potential consequences do you see?
Who has a different proposal?
What arguments do you have in its favour?
What do you think of the arguments?
What do the arguments mean for your position?
Do you want to change your opinion based on the arguments made?
Do you see any other consequences?
Are there any new proposals?
Are there any new arguments?

7 I propose that we cast our votes. Agreed?

Decision-making

8 Who is in favour of X's proposal? (Give the name of the attendee who made the proposal).
Who is in favour of Y's proposal?
And so on.

Finalising

9 Who will finalise what, and for when?

10 Continue on with the next item on the agenda (point 3)

SDMI meeting model®	Explanation
1a, 1b and 1c Minutes on the previous meeting Announcements Any other business	These points are the fixed agenda items, meaning that 'any other business' is handled at the start of the meeting. Usually a provisional agenda is made prior to the meeting. When submitting the agenda point, the submitter gives a time estimate.
2a Determining the definitive agenda Any additions to the provisional agenda?	At point 2a, the provisional agenda is supplemented with items that have arisen during point 1. Once the preliminary agenda is complete, a check can be made to see whether the agreed meeting time allows enough time to deal with all the points on the agenda. If so, go to point 3. If not, continue with point 2b.
2b In the event of an excess of agenda items: proposals for postponement, impose time limits for agenda items, extend the duration of the meeting.	At the meeting, the person who submitted the topic determines whether his agenda item can perhaps be postponed or have less time devoted to it. If the meeting time is extended, this can only be done if everyone's consent is obtained.
3, 4 and 5 Which question or suggestion do you want to deal with? What was the reason for this? Goal of raising the issue (decision, advice, information)	Once the agenda is fixed, the agenda items are dealt with one by one. The person who introduced the topic answers questions 3, 4 and 5 for that topic.
6 Discussion, solution-oriented questions: What is your proposal, arguments, pros and cons, consequences?	This point lists questions that the chair and the participants can use to help to structure and bring depth to the discussion. The proposals made during the discussion are recorded. A list is made of all proposals mentioned.
7 Is everyone able to cast their vote?	At this point, a check is made to see whether every attendee is able to cast his or her vote. If so, then the meeting proceeds to voting on the proposals. If not, then the meeting will look at what is required in order to be able to make a decision at a later time. A team member may not yet be able to examine all the potential consequences of a proposal, or may require time to gather more information.

>>

>>

SDMI meeting model®	Explanation
8 All proposals are put to the vote, one by one. Who is in favour of the proposal?	The votes are cast during this point. All proposals that have been made in relation to the relevant agenda item are put to the vote, and each team member can vote for multiple proposals. This makes it easier to reach a consensus. If a team member has no preference, or conversely is not opposed to a particular idea, then the best option is to vote in favour of a proposal. Ultimately, of course, the aim is to come to decisions that are workable for everyone.
9 Who will finalise what, and for when?	Finalizing of the agenda items is organized now. Agreements are made about who will deal with what, and by what date.
10 Can we move on to the next item?	At this point, the chair introduces the following agenda item.

9 Dealing with conflict

Peace is not the absence of conflict, but the ability to cope with conflict by peaceful means.
– Ronald Reagan –

Dealing with disagreements and conflicts in a self-managing team calls for a particular approach. There is no boss in charge, ready to step in and solve problems at the most difficult points. The team members are responsible for everything, including sorting out any differences of opinion. They have to work things out together, possibly with their coach's help.

Differences of opinion don't have to mean that there's a problem, and a difference of opinion isn't immediately a conflict. Obviously team members can think differently about a subject, and they then meet to discuss workable solutions. Different points of view can end up resulting in better decisions.

It becomes more difficult when team members cling on to their opinions and aren't prepared to compromise. Differences in cultural background, education or character can also mean that team members don't always understand each other, sometimes leading to differences of opinion that are difficult to resolve.

This can result in gossip, colleagues being ignored, and the formation of sub-groups, which then in turn leads to emotions running high.

Some organizations use rules or training to try to avoid these types of situations. Training can indeed help to make people more aware of their behaviour, but over time team members often fall back into old habits.

Even self-managing organizations experience conflicts. In this chapter we give suggestions based on the SDMI®, to assist team members, coaches and managers in dealing with conflict-based situations. Because if conflicts can't be avoided, then you need to know how to deal with them.

WHAT IS A CONFLICT?

Conflicts have to do with *differences of opinion*. But in order for a conflict to be a problem, the conflicting parties need to have something in common – otherwise you would just shrug your shoulders and walk away. Within an organization, that common interest is usually the fact that you work on a team together and depend on each other to be able to carry out your duties.

Differences of opinion are not by definition a source of conflict. They also offer opportunities to take a different approach to problem-solving, which can improve the quality of the work. However, this is conditional on both parties being prepared to consider the value of the other's opinion. The word 'conflict' would scarcely occur to anyone in this type of situation.

However, this situation can lead to conflict when a team member is *not prepared to give in*. This causes *emotions* to rise. Conflict situations in self-managing teams can be recognised by a number of characteristics, including laborious decision-making processes. Consensus is difficult or impossible to reach, discussions are chaotic and emotional, and team members try to 'clip each other's wings'. The team members with the most informal power end up determining the agreements. The others vote for those choices 'for the sake of peace'.

This type of conflict-heavy atmosphere in a team is very stressful and often unhealthy for the team members. It also tends to have a negative influence on the quality of the work.

SDMI®, A TOOL FOR HANDLING CONFLICTS

A great deal has been written about conflict and the various ways of handling it. It has been stated that it's good to know what kind of conflict you are dealing with; one conflict-solving format is based on the distinction between instrumental conflicts, scarcity conflicts, social-emotional conflicts, or power struggles.

Courses in conflict management give insight into the way the student solves conflicts. They distinguish between avoidance, forcing, giving in, trying to find a compromise, and solving the problem.

The trouble with distinguishing between types of conflict and conflict styles is that no conflict or conflict style fits into one single category; in practice things are always a bit more unruly.

For this reason the SDMI® (see Chapter 7) also doesn't distinguish between different types of conflicts and doesn't describe conflict styles. Instead, it aims to offer concrete ways to handle conflict.

CONFLICTS WITHIN THE TEAM

Conflict within a self-managing team is very difficult for the team members: it takes up a lot of energy, it brings up unpleasant emotions such as anger and sadness, it affects the atmosphere in the team and, last but not least, it usually has a negative effect on the quality of the work. In addition, conflicts within the team are difficult because there's no manager with the power to 'take action' against a colleague. Not that the manager ever actually did so, but having him there gave the team the opportunity to grumble about and to the supervisor; that creates a bond.

Self-managing team members share responsibility and when things aren't going well, they need to talk to each other about it. If the problems aren't resolved, the conflict persists. There is then a great deal of chat (and grumbling) amongst the group, and a risk of the conflict escalating. Some team members may find this extremely stressful, resulting in illness and absenteeism, or some colleagues feeling the need to look for another job.

It's therefore extremely important that employees in a self-managing team find a way to handle conflict situations constructively.

But first: what types of situations can cause a difference of opinion to degenerate into a conflict? Here are some examples.

- A team member refuses to budge and is not prepared to consider other opinions.

- Team members are being bullied by one or more colleagues. For example, they are constantly assigned to unpopular shifts, they are informed of things too late so that they can't do the work properly, they're confronted with appointments scheduled for times at which they're not available, they don't receive replies to their emails, and so on.
- Team members who are disqualified. This is reflected in statements such as: 'You can't do that, so we didn't involve you', 'Just leave that task to Peter, I don't think it's suitable for you', 'The question is whether it's a good idea for you to study that, it does require a certain level ...', or 'I'll do that, you're not able to do it.'
- A team member takes charge of the team. He makes decisions without involving the other team members ('That client happened to call me, and I've made the agreement with them that we do not have time in the next two months').
- A team member keeps the team tasks to herself and when it's time to rotate tasks, says: 'I've been doing this task for so long now, if someone else has to do it then it will take them a long time to get the hang of it.' This is usually done with tasks which enable the team member to have a great deal of influence on the team's performance.
- A team member doesn't take her colleagues' capacity into account. She regularly allows others to go above and beyond their contracts or to work overtime, without considering what those colleagues are actually able to manage. She ignores her overtaxed colleagues' requests for the work to be organized differently.

CONFORMING TO BASIC AGREEMENTS

In all of these examples, the basis for the conflict lies in a lack of respect for people with differing opinions. Some people are unable or unwilling to consider their colleagues' wants and needs, and that is a prerequisite for being able to work constructively as part of a self-managing team. If it doesn't work, or when there's someone who's not prepared to do his best to achieve it, then that's the end of that.

One of the first questions in conflicts like the ones described above is: are you prepared to co-operate in making team agreements, can you muster respect for your colleagues when their opinions are different from yours, and are you prepared to work within the organizational frameworks?

The initial answer will usually be 'yes'. However, regular evaluations should be held to determine whether this is actually happening in practice, and that doesn't always happen. If it's repeatedly apparent that someone isn't able to comply with these agreements, that colleague will be asked to seek a job at another organization.

RAISING THE ISSUE OF A CONFLICT IN THE TEAM

The question is obviously: 'How do team members bring up conflicts?' Even touching on issues such as those above can have unpleasant consequences. The person causing the conflict will immediately see the discussion as an attack on his dominant position, and may well apply even more pressure and demonstrate unpleasant behaviour. Addressing conflicts therefore requires a certain amount of courage.

Communicating in terms of what you want can help. It starts with knowing exactly what you want and why (goal), as well as the powers that you and the other party possess (position).

For example: 'Mark, I'd like it if you would only accept new clients when we have all been able to discuss it during the meeting, and have been able to make a joint decision. Can we agree to that?'

Expressing what you'd like to change in this way means that it doesn't come across as a reproach. In addition there probably won't be any annoyance in your voice, which is often enough to cause a difficult discussion.

If Mark says 'no', then you're already at the point where you can discuss the core of the conflict. Mark doesn't want to work within the framework of 'team decisions are made by consensus'. If he says 'yes', then you've made an agreement that you can remind Mark about if he continues to make decisions on his own.

Many colleagues find it difficult to address others about their behaviour. The behaviour that they need to address the colleagues about is not experienced as positive (otherwise you wouldn't need to speak to them about it), and that same problematic behaviour means that bringing it up with your colleague will probably land you in a heap of trouble. All in all, addressing conflict-causing colleagues about their behaviour is extremely unappealing. Many team members would prefer to look for another job than to get into a 'fight'. Others simply make the best of the situation, but they don't enjoy their work at all.

Despite this, it's important to have the conversation – not addressing the issue only makes the conflict harder to resolve. If, on the other hand, the conflict *is* successfully resolved as a result of the discussion, mutual trust increases and the quality of the teamwork along with it.

Here, too, you can make your wishes known: 'Sarah, in future could you please not make negative comments about me or other colleagues, because it can be harmful to us and our team?' Sarah will probably deny or justify her behaviour by saying that she doesn't do that or she doesn't have a choice, but she will still agree with the request. After all, it's a reasonable one: making negative comments about colleagues goes against all rules of decency, and Sarah is well aware of that. Every time she makes negative comments about others, you can approach her about it: 'Sarah, remember we made an agreement?'

Using the points given in the SDMI®, teams can go a long way towards being able to discuss conflict situations and perhaps even solving them.

HELP FROM THE COACH

When conflicts are stubborn and more complex, team members usually find it very difficult to arrive at good, workable agreements. In such cases, it's ideal for self-managing teams to be able to ask a team coach for help (Chapter 5 has more information on this). The coach is impartial and has expertise in dealing with teamwork situations and issues. She's not a member of the team, so it's easier for her to address tricky issues. Her involvement can help to move a team conflict past an impasse.

It's easier for a coach to tell Mark (see previous paragraph) that there's no place for him on a self-managing team if he continues to make team decisions on his own. Team members can say the same thing, but it's easier for the coach as she doesn't have a colleague-level working relationship with the team members.

IMPROVEMENT PLAN

When someone who causes conflicts indicates that he does want to improve, the coach encourages the team to agree on an improvement plan: what exactly do the team members expect of each other, what specific agreements should be made, and how will these agreements be evaluated? Obviously, this process should result in an improved situation – if it doesn't, then the plan can be adapted. If the plan still doesn't bring about improvements, the team can discuss the implications this has for the team members.

THE MANAGER'S ROLE IN CONFLICTS

Once a conflict reaches the point that there's no way to solve it other than dismissing a team member, then the manager comes into the picture. The team members and the coach are not authorized to dismiss the team member; that power rests with the manager.

In our example, the team asks the manager to dismiss team member Mark, using the information in the improvement plan (the file) to support the dismissal. The manager examines the file and determines whether there are sufficient legal grounds for the dismissal. In other words: has enough been done to try to reach agreement, and has the employee had sufficient opportunity to improve or to learn to change his attitude towards the team?

If not, then the manager asks the team to do these things, and lets them know what additional information is needed for the file. He may also choose to meet with the team in order to see whether there are still opportunities for improvement. If he spots these, he will advise the team to ask the coach for help (again) when they continue with the improvement plan.

CAREFUL PROCESS

If the manager sees no hope for improvement and believes that everything in the file is in order, he can begin the dismissal procedure. This is not a rapid process. These types of processes must be carried out with care, and that takes time. Causing unnecessary harm to a team member is obviously something to be avoided. Some conflict situations drag on for years and become so confused that it's very difficult to identify a 'guilty' party.

In addition, there are not always good reports on all discussions. In order to avoid differences in interpretation, it may be wise to make new agreements.

This is one of the reasons why the causes of conflict are not sought out when working with the SDMI®: the causes are often no longer identifiable, and everyone has their own interpretation of the truth.

It's better to make workable agreements based on the current situation, and to evaluate these, regardless of 'how this could have come about'. It will automatically be obvious who's responsible for disrupting the process of collaboration. Everyone has to agree on the agreements so there is support within the team, even from those who have apparently been unable or unwilling to comply with the agreements.

Experience shows that if the process is carefully supervised and every team member feels that they've been taken seriously, people are more inclined to accept responsibility for the outcome and, for example, look for another job, without the situation having to end in a lawsuit. The organization might even help the employee to find suitable employment elsewhere.

PERSONALITY CLASHES

Many conflicts arise from the fact that people's characters are simply not a good fit with each other: there's a personality clash. People don't 'get' each other, and despite the team members doing their best, the collaboration is unsuccessful. Mary thinks that she's saying something to Tom in a friendly way, but Tom automatically goes on the defensive because he thinks that she's blaming him for anything and everything. Mary of course responds to that, and they end up in yet another argument.

If that is the underlying cause of the conflict, then the team can make as many agreements as they like with the aim of improving co-operation, but it won't make much of a difference to the situation. In such cases it might be better if one or more team members are able to move to another team within the organization. If the quality of the work is good, it would be a shame for the organization to lose these employees.

This is a task for the coach. If team members want to move to a new team due to conflict, then the members of the new team will be on their guard: What kind of people are joining our team? Why didn't it work out on that team, and why would it work well on ours? Things are going so well on our team ... Other teams often see the person who's leaving a team as someone who is unable to co-operate.

When making preparations for the transfer, the coach can do a lot to promote a positive image. People are often afraid to be open about the reason for the transfer, because that would infringe on employees' privacy. But if you make an agreement in advance with the person who would like to transfer to another team on what you will say about the reasons for this, then obviously you're not infringing their privacy.

The reasons are often very plausible:

- the team member really likes to work in a very structured environment, and the current team didn't see the need for that;
- the team member enjoys working on complex tasks and wanted to do that type of work himself, but the other team members wanted to do it too. In another team, people might be very happy to have someone who likes doing the difficult tasks;
- the team member is used to communicating very directly, and the other team members were not happy with it. It may well be that the new team communicates differently, and would very much appreciate that direct style.

If the coach holds an exploratory meeting with the new team to see whether the team member might be a good fit, the discussion with the new team member will proceed without preconceptions.

DEALING WITH EMOTIONS

One of the things that characterises a conflict is high emotions. By emotions we mean sadness, fear, anger and happiness. The last of these usually doesn't cause problems, but the first three can be quite difficult to deal with.

Obviously we always feel emotions, but as a rule they're not so strong that they cause us problems. When it comes to happy emotions, we can't get enough of them. We're never really sure what to say to people who are grieving, and we're often scared of angry people. Anxious people should just stop making such a fuss: 'There's nothing to be scared of – come on, get over it!'

People can be very hurtful when emotions are running high, and then later – once the dust has settled – they often sincerely regret it. But by then the words have been spoken and the relationship has already been affected. Team spirit can be quite seriously damaged by the emotions of a few team members. So how can you deal with emotions constructively?

Some communication techniques advocate talking about emotions. Comments like 'I can see that that makes you very sad; do you want to talk about it?', or 'I saw your expression change – how did you feel when he said that to you?', and 'I felt that you froze when John made that comment, but you didn't say anything. What are you trying to hide?' draw attention to emotions. When you pay a lot of attention to something, it grows, so the emotion isn't reduced – it increases. That's not always desirable – particularly in work situations, people want to be able to have a 'normal' conversation without being overcome by emotion.

Once you start paying more attention to the content of the discussion and less to the emotions, the emotion usually automatically becomes less intense. You can draw attention to the content of the discussion by asking questions that require a bit of thinking, for example, 'What do you think needs to change in the way you talk to each other about mistakes?' Focusing your energy on thinking leaves there's no energy to sustain the emotion and it automatically lessens.

Emotions, especially anger and rage, can mean that people in a discussion have less understanding for each other's points of view. Not because they are asking unreasonable things from each other, but because the other person's aggression has an effect on them, and the situation becomes even harder to change. It's therefore important to avoid increasing the emotion.

Emotions are usually expressed non-verbally and are mostly visible in posture, facial expressions and the voice. When this is done in aggressively you feel attacked and automatically go on the defence. Your response will be emotional too, and will quite possibly not be an effective way to address the substance of the problem.

If you listen carefully to what is being *said* and are able to ignore the non-verbal behaviour, the emotion will be less of a problem. You will feel less attacked and will be less likely to respond emotionally. Focusing on what's being said also makes it easier to respond with a substance-focused reply. By asking questions that make the other person think, you may also be able to reduce their level of emotion. The ultimate aim is to enable the people involved to have a constructive discussion.

DIFFERENCES OF OPINION DON'T HAVE TO BE RESOLVED

We tend to assume that it's important to resolve conflicts or differences of opinion, but it's not always possible, such as in cases where consensus can't be reached on a single proposal. Further investigation sometimes shows that all parties may well have valid arguments for sticking with their own point of view.

In this type of situation, it can be a good idea to discuss the consequences of allowing the difference of opinion to stand. When doing something like helping dyslexic students, or dressing wounds, or working on the acquisition of new clients, a team will regularly discuss (or argue about) whether they should be following method X or method Y. When differences of opinion are allowed to stand, every team member uses the method that suits him or her best. This means different methods are used alongside each other within a team. The team members can conclude that this is actually not a problem, and it's therefore not necessary to discuss it.

THE COACH AND DEALING WITH CONFLICTS

The team often asks for assistance from the coach at times when they can't sort things out for themselves, so she is regularly confronted with conflict situations. Chapter 5 describes the intervention options that the coach has when following the SDMI®. In principle she can use these to deal with any situation.

In this section we would like to go into more detail about the situation that arises when some team members are willing to discuss an issue, and others are not. Many coaches say that the 'shuttle strategy' is useful here. The following gives an example of how it can be applied.

Shuttle strategy

Conflict sometimes progress to the point that team members are no longer prepared to sit at the table with each other to discuss it. The work still gets done, but people only carry out their own tasks and only essential communication takes place. A few of the team members might ask you, their coach, to help, or perhaps you take the initiative to see whether the conflict can be resolved. What do you do?

You might be tempted to get the parties to come to the table, because if *that* succeeds, they will also be happy to discuss the conflict. However, bringing the parties together can take a lot of time and energy from both the coach and the team. There is also the risk of the conflicting parties turning against you, their coach. *You* want them to focus on each other. When they sit down at the table together, they might focus on you and if you're not careful, you'll be drawn into the conflict too! You can also take the team members' decision seriously and *not* make any effort to bring them together, but instead just get to work with the parties separately. What you then do is shuttle backwards and forwards between the parties and, through you, they can say what they want to say to their colleagues. A conversation with a team member might proceed as follows:

James: 'Well, I'm not talking to her any more. Someone else will just have to do it.'

Coach: 'I could talk to her on your behalf.'

James: 'That sounds like a good idea. Then you can see for yourself the crazy things she says.'

Coach: 'Maybe so. What do you want me to say to Sarah?'

James: 'That she can't gossip about me to our other colleagues any more. She's giving everyone a bad impression of me. People are starting to avoid me. They're going to start asking me questions and I've noticed that I'm starting to feel like an outsider. Then later on I hear things like that she's organized a team lunch on my day off. It's just not workable any more. It's slowly got to the stage where it's really "either she goes, or I do".'

Coach (taking up pen and paper): 'Can I tell it to her like that?'

James: 'Well, that's probably a little harsh. Just say that I don't like the way she talks about me to other people.'

Coach (writes the sentence down word for word, so that James can see her writing it): 'What else do you want me to say to her?'

James: 'That thanks to her behaviour, I feel like an outsider on the team, and that doesn't feel good.'

Coach (writes that sentence down too): 'OK, what else do you want to say?'

James: 'These are the most important things.'

The coach plans a meeting with Sarah and tells her what James wants to say to her. When she's talking to Sarah, too, the coach regularly asks: 'What shall I say to James?'

This allows you to bring the conflict partners in contact with each other. Here, too, it's important that you as a coach don't judge what's being said. A comment like 'Yes, but Sarah, you can't say that to James!' means that you are interfering in the conflict. Writing down, and perhaps reading aloud, what you're going to say means that the message that you're conveying remains the responsibility of the conflict partners.

STEP BY STEP CONFLICT RESOLUTION PLAN

When the team members or the coach are faced with a conflict situation, it can be a good idea to follow a procedure with a number of steps to work through. It doesn't matter which phase the conflict has reached, or which category it fits into. The SDMI® doesn't define or categorise conflicts. You choose your interventions based on the five points which we described earlier.

The following steps can be used as a guideline.

1 *Determining the objective(s)*
It's already been said: without a goal, you can't get started. Sometimes determining your goal or goals can take quite a long time. We're dealing with conflicts, and when it comes to these, the team members' goals are often contradictory. The trick is then to formulate a shared goal, so that it can be used as a basis for making workable joint agreements. When Richard and Elizabeth have definite ideas about how the training budget should be distributed but the other team members don't subscribe to those ideas, there are probably contradictory goals at play. The joint goal might then be for every team member to be happy with the budget distribution. If Richard and Elizabeth support that goal, the next question might be: 'How can we reach a satisfactory distribution?' If it turns out that Richard and Elizabeth don't want to take their colleagues' wishes and interests into account, they clearly don't share the joint goal of 'being happy with the distribution of the training budget'. If they don't want to alter their goal, then you can't make an agreement and you go on to step 6. If they do want to take their colleagues' wishes into account, you can go to step 2. It may be that you need a number of meetings to either formulate a common goal, or realise that it isn't going to work.

2 *Agreements that are essential in order to arrive at a workable situation*
If you are able to reach agreement on the goal in step 1, you can often make the agreements that will lead to achieving the goal. It is then important to discuss the consequences of not fulfilling the agreements. In the example from step 1, the agreement might be that you will only work on the agreements that everyone has approved. Richard and Elizabeth are then committed to

examining other people's reasons and will need to do their best to make it pleasing to their colleagues.

3 *Agree on a period during which the agreement will be worked on*

4 *The agreements can be evaluated if desired*

5 *When agreements are not honoured: make new agreements, or discuss consequences*
Once some time has passed and after working with the agreements, it may be that the team members discover that it's (still) not workable. Perhaps a possible improvement will be identified, which may provide the impetus to make new agreements. In that case, you start again at step 2. It may also turn out that the goals need to be adapted, and then you go back to step 1. It might even be that at this stage the team discovers that the goal is still not endorsed by everyone. In our example: Richard and Elizabeth don't want to take their teammates' interests into account. The group then discusses whether or not other agreements could be made, so that the decisions can be made as a team.

6 *No workable agreement possible*
Ultimately it may turn out that the parties are not able to reach an agreement, that no workable agreements can be made, or that time after time these are not honoured. It may be that the team just leaves things as they are. If this is no longer workable, the coach can advise the team to ask the manager to handle the conflict.

10 In closing ... Frequently Asked Questions

In this book we have tried to give the fullest possible picture of what we mean by self-management, as well as what's involved in the transition from hierarchy to self-management.

Our work involves assisting the boards of various types of organizations to realise a form of self-management suited to their specific situation. We also train coaches, team members and supporting staff, building up their skills to make them more effective within self-managing organizations. We do this across a variety of businesses, from health care organizations, educational and municipal institutions, through to bakery chains, technical wholesalers and travel companies, both in the Netherlands and abroad.

We hear many questions about self-management from these very varied backgrounds; here are a few of them.

1 To what extent do you involve the team members during the introduction phase? And to what extent is this *real* participation? Or do you not actually give them any control?

2 Many employees are resistant to the changes – how can you prevent this?

3 Can you set up a working group to prepare for a change in the self-managing organization?

4 What do you do when a team doesn't want to take responsibility for its own organizational tasks? For example when a team doesn't want to do their own rosters?

5 As a manager, what do you do when a team doesn't step up to its responsibilities?

6 As a manager, how do you keep on top of the team members' ups and downs?

7 How does the manager ensure that he's doing a good job? In other words: who takes care of the manager?

8 When do you pull the plug on a team?

9 What role do the staff play in innovation? Some employees in staff functions sometimes complain about team members: 'If it was up to the teams, we'd still be writing with pencil and paper.'

10 Do the staff members also need to be organized as a self-managing team?

11 Do you need to include the staff members in the changes right from when you first begin to introduce self-management?

12 What does a staff member do when he notices that the team isn't working properly within the organizational frameworks?

13 What should a staff member do if he doesn't receive details (for example records) from the team members on time?

14 Who do you treat like staff? The team? Or the individual team member who carries out the team task in the field in which the staff member works?

15 The staff member observes the same problem in a number of teams. How should he handle this within the organization?

16 What's important for a team when they first start self-management? What do they talk about?

17 What can the coach do when a self-organizing team first gets started?

18 Are you still a self-managing organization if you train the team leaders in coaching management, and give the team more control?

19 Can you go back to being a hierarchy if self-management isn't successful?

20 If self-management is too difficult, can a team temporarily go back to working with a manager?

21 Do all employees always want self-management?

22 What do you do when a team doesn't step up to its responsibilities, and doesn't do its best to work well?

23 What does being responsible actually mean?

24 Why is the team meeting so important?

Many of these questions can be broken down to the basic principles: how should we best serve the interests of our clients and of the primary process? And do these decisions fit within the organizational frameworks?

The key here is always that management, supporting staff, and team members, all in their own fields, work with each other and try to work things out together. The biggest danger that has the potential to undermine self-organization is that organization members might start thinking for each other, regardless of whether it's a for-profit or non-profit organization.

This book contains a number of examples of choices which have been made in real-life situations, but every situation is different and deserves to have self-management tailored to its own specific requirements.

If you can't find the answer to the questions raised above, or to your own questions about self-management – or perhaps you just don't want to have to search through the entire book again – then send us an email: zelfsturing@ivs-opleidingen.nl.

We are happy to chat with you to discuss the most suitable answer for your situation.

Astrid Vermeer and Ben Wenting

FURTHER READING

Organizational Innovation by Integrating Simplification. Learning from Buurtzorg Nederland (2014)
Sharda S. Nandram. ISBN 9783319117249

Reinventing organizations (2014)
Frederic Laloux. ISBN 9782960133509

Coachen van zelfsturende teams. Hoe doe je dat? (2013) (Dutch)
Astrid Vermeer and Ben Wenting. ISBN 9789035235748

Zelfsturende teams in de praktijk (2012/2014) (Dutch)
Astrid Vermeer and Ben Wenting. ISBN 9789035238312

Zelfsturing, hoe het wél werkt (2016) (Dutch)
Astrid Vermeer and Ben Wenting. ISBN 9789035249059

Printed in Poland
by Amazon Fulfillment
Poland Sp. z o.o., Wrocław

51956460R00094